Football
Hooligans

First published in 2013

A catalogue record for this book is available from the British Library

ISBN: 978-0-85733-190-8

Published by Haynes Publishing, Sparkford, Yeovil,
Somerset BA22 7JJ, UK
Tel: 01963 442030 Fax: 01963 440001
Int. tel: +44 1963 442030 Int. fax: +44 1963 440001
E-mail: sales@haynes.co.uk
Website: www.haynes.co.uk

Haynes North America Inc., 861 Lawrence Drive, Newbury Park, California 91320, USA

Images © Mirrorpix

Creative Director: Kevin Gardner
Designed for Haynes by BrainWave

Printed and bound in the US

Football
Hooligans

From The Case Files of

THE PEOPLE and DAILY Mirror

Claire Welch

Contents

Introduction   1

1906 – Sheffield Football Riot   27

1909 – Angry Scenes at Football Riot in Glasgow   29

1912 – Irish Football Riot: Spectators Rush the Field   32

1958 – City Seeks Control of Pitches: Action against
Soccer Rowdies   33

1959 – Arsenal–Colchester Cup Match   35

1964 – Busby Team Quits Train to Take the Coach   37

1965 – British Sports Appalled by Barbaric
Behaviour of Rome   42

1967 – "Let's Birch the Soccer Rowdies"   44

1971 – More calls to "Bring back the Birch"
for Soccer Hooligans   46

1972 – Soccer Fans Riot in Streets   47

1973 – Soccer Rowdies Sleep in Jail   50

1974 – Soccer Rioter Jailed and the "Battle of Brum"   57

1975 – TV Starts to Play its Part   69

1976 – Pubs Call Time on the Thugs   77

1982 – Tears for the Man of Peace   79

1983 – Grinning Soccer Thug is Freed   84

1984 – While Another is Sent to Jail   85

1985 – "They're Going to Get You, Mr Leftley"   88

1986 – Football is Back ... so are the Hooligans   121

1987 – Non-drinking, Chess-playing Birdwatcher is
Named Thug   132

1988 – Britain's Clean Up Soccer Campaign   135

1990 – British Sports Minister "Puts the Boot In"   140

1992 – New Flare-up as England Face Ban   142

1995 – Lansdowne Road: Yobs Make War on Peace   145

1997 – Brian Reade, Hitting Where It Hurt   168

1998 – British Football Yobs Named in an Attempt to Avoid Disaster   171

1999 – Soccer Movie Murder Link   197

2000 – UEFA's Complacency Brings Back Chilling Memories   200

2001 – Lout of Range   204

2002 – England v Poland and that's Just the Picture   206

2003 – UEFA's Reputation in Tatters   213

2004 – Girl of 14 Imprisoned   215

2010 – MacIntyre "Bar Fight"   217

2013 – And Finally ... Football Hooligan Becomes a Woman   218

Introduction

British football fans have a shocking record for violence. In 1972, Glasgow Rangers were suspended from European football after supporters rioted in Barcelona. Between then and the mid-1990s, hooligans blackened Britain's name many times. In 1974, Tottenham were barred from playing their next two European matches at White Hart Lane after fans rioted during the UEFA Cup final second-leg tie in Rotterdam. The following year, Leeds United were banned for four seasons from European competition following riots by their supporters in Paris. The ban was cut to two years after a successful appeal. In 1977, Manchester United were withdrawn from the European Cup Winners' Cup after crowd trouble in a first-round match in Saint-Étienne. The club were later reinstated, but were ordered to play their home ties at least 125 miles from Manchester. In October 1977, England fans caused about £18,000-worth of damage in what the newspapers described as a "Trail of Terror". Luxembourg said at the time that if they were drawn against England they would forfeit the match.

Then, in 1980, England were fined £30,000 after fans rioted in Turin during the European Championship match against Belgium. Police moved in with tear gas to halt trouble during the England v Belgium match. In June 1981, 13 English fans were deported after riots in Basle, in which three English fans were stabbed. Later, 23 were arrested after a pub brawl, which left three more fans in hospital. Then, in 1982, Manchester United fans rioted in the Valencia stadium after their side were beaten 1-2 in a UEFA Cup match. That same year, an English fan was stabbed in the heart in Spain during heated fighting between English and Spanish hooligans at the World Cup. It didn't stop there. In September 1982, sporadic violence in Copenhagen, Denmark, broke out. Fans brought further disgrace to the image of the English football fan abroad. Fourteen months later, in Luxembourg, trouble in Ostend spilt into the principality where England were to play a European Championship qualifier. One local man was stabbed and 13 fans were arrested. France was the next country to suffer when riot police were forced to attack in Parc des Princes, following a "friendly" where English fans charged a small group of French supporters in February 1984. A Tottenham fan was shot dead in Brussels and the police held 200 fans in custody. Some of the worst ever violence happened inside a European ground in Brussels in May 1985. This catastrophic event, at the Heysel stadium, resulted in 39 deaths, with 350 left injured, as Liverpool and Juventus followers clashed before the European Cup. After this, English clubs were banned indefinitely from Europe.

In September 1987, nine were arrested in Germany before a "friendly" international in Düsseldorf. More than 7,000 fans had travelled to the match and most were described as "well behaved". Back in Germany in June 1988, two nights of violence occurred in Stuttgart during European Championships. The violence was triggered by an England defeat by Ireland. The then prime minister, Margaret Thatcher, had little choice but to call an emergency soccer summit. The following year in September 1989, 100 English fans went on the rampage in Stockholm, Sweden, where passers-by were attacked and stores looted. More than 100 arrests were made, and 82 fans were held in custody before being deported. The story was no better in 1990 when English fans – again on the rampage – caused chaos in Sardinia, Italy, in June. The worst violence was seen in Rimini against Dutch supporters. It resulted in around 246 hooligans being deported. Two years later, two nights of violence in Malmö and Stockholm in Sweden took place at the European Championships. More than 1,000 riot police were drafted in to quell violence as 70 supporters went on the rampage. Three were arrested. In 1993, in Oslo, Norway, there was more fighting between English and Norwegian fans in the city centre. However, the match did go ahead trouble-free. In October that same year, mounted police charged 300 bottle-throwing hooligans in Amsterdam, Holland. Bars and cafés were smashed, while even worse violence occurred in Rotterdam. The authorities deported 431 hooligans. In 1995, a friendly against Ireland, in Dublin, saw the match abandoned after 27 minutes as England fans ran riot. A riot in Trafalgar Square, London, ensued in 1996 after Germany beat England in the Euro 96 semi-final. In 1998, there was more rampaging by English fans in Marseille, France, while later that year almost 100 England fans were arrested and deported before a European Championship match in Luxembourg.

It seemed that the 21st century would not remain unaffected by these thugs when, in 2000, 19 fans were hurt, five seriously, while a further 19 were arrested in Copenhagen. That same year, 584 England fans were arrested following riots in Brussels and Charleroi during Euro 2000. In 2001, 20 English fans were arrested in Frankfurt and Munich before World Cup qualifiers. Two England fans were shot at the Euro 2004 qualifier in Bratislava, Slovakia, in 2003, and, in the same year, three England fans were shot and two were stabbed before the World Cup qualifier in Zurich. But is football violence a state of affairs that started in the 1970s and peaked in the 1980s? Not according to research.

"Cometh have a go if thou thinks thou art hard enough," read the "Olde Footy Aggro" heading in the *Mirror* in January 2004. Journalist Matthew Cooper was writing about the history of football hooliganism, which was making trouble long before the Inter City Firm and the Headhunters arrived. In fact, soccer violence was around in the 1600s, "about 350 years before its 1980s peak, according to a professor's research," wrote Cooper. Bernard Capp stated that football in the 17th century was a seasonal activity, often played between villages at Easter or on Shrove Tuesday. However, when the Puritans took power after the Civil War, they banned disorderly sports and festive celebrations. Professor Capp, of Warwick University, told how Canterbury's mayor abolished Christmas in 1647. Crowds responded by bringing out footballs as a symbol of festive mayhem. The game became a "flashpoint for social and political tensions". The Puritans' insistence on observing the Sabbath did not help, as football was often played on Sundays. The professor added: "This triggered open conflict. Church records cite frequent confrontations, with footballers playing in the churchyard itself."

In 1968, the problem of football "rowdies", as they were then known, was to be probed by a Government working party, which included top soccer officials. The inquiry was the idea of Sports

Minister Denis Howell, who hoped that it would result in useful suggestions on how to combat football hooliganism before the next season's kick-off. Sir John Lang, the Government's then adviser on sport, was set to chair the inquiry and its 12-strong working party, which, in addition to Football Association and League officials, also represented professional footballers. Among the issues to be probed were match arrangements and crowd control, alongside how best to use supporters' clubs and improved seating. The following year it was announced that soccer fans might be offered free train tickets in return for acting as "police" on football "specials". The plan, suggested at a conference on football hooliganism in October 1969, called for supporters' clubs to provide teams of vigilantes. The vigilantes would wear special armbands and would patrol trains on the lookout for troublemakers. They would be unpaid, but British Railways was willing to give them free tickets to travel. Delegates at the conference, called by the then home secretary, James Callaghan, in an effort to curb the growing menace of hooliganism, were reported to be keen on the plan. Representatives of the police, Home Office officials and football organizations were all called to the conference in London. Delegates included Football Association secretary Denis Follows and the secretary of the National Federation of Football Supporters' Clubs, Archie Gooch. A Home Office spokesman said, following the conference: "This was a preliminary meeting. There will be more after the delegates have reported back to their own people." Suggestions had "ranged over a wide area," he said. Later, police chiefs from all over Britain met transport police representatives to discuss crowd violence and plans to reinforce the transport police on soccer "specials".

However, the trouble was far from over, and in 1974 newspapers warned: "Wake up you Soccer clubs before it's too late – and give the real fan a passport to peace on the terraces." In August that year came the reckoning, when the police courts were full of the type of fans the clubs didn't want. The "teenage terrorists", or "rowdies", from Manchester United, Arsenal, Crystal Palace, Leicester, Stoke and Middlesbrough were said to be the worst offenders. The newspaper article in the *Mirror* stated: "But, the honest citizen and the decent fan is entitled when he reads of the crimes and punishments of the hooligans to ask what the hell Soccer is doing itself to purge the game of this criminal element?" There was no way that clubs could escape their responsibilities, condemned the journalist writing the piece. He stated that it was no good "wringing their hands in woe". The comment made by Tommy Docherty of Manchester United was perhaps typical of those of all his fellow managers. He said: "These are not supporters. They are followers. We don't want them. If there is anything I can do or say to stamp out this hooliganism, I will. But there appears no answer to it." The newspaper's journalist – whose name is undisclosed – disagreed with Tommy Docherty and said: "There is, Tommy. And it comes to me in a letter from Alex Johnston of Cannock Road, Wolverhampton, who is chairman of the 20,000-strong National Union of Football Supporters. He writes: 'The membership card is the only foolproof system I know to cure hooliganism inside and outside all football grounds. I wrote to every club and all the important people in the League and the FA before this season began. Any fan causing trouble would have his identity card taken from him and would thus be banned from Soccer for the rest of the season. It needs only one club to adopt the scheme, and the others would have to follow.' I think it is worth a trial," wrote the journalist. The idea of a social contract between the real supporter and the club they supported, really did appeal. The *Mirror* journalist continued: "I think League clubs should be brave enough to offer a seat on the Board to a representative of their Official Supporters' Club, in return for his help in cleaning up the terraces."

The alternative, at the time, was what was happening to London teenager, John Moran. He was arrested when some Manchester United fans ran amok in Ostend. Despite protesting his innocence, he was held in a Bruges cell measuring 10ft by 5ft, with no running water. All Moran was able to do was watch through a small window as holidaymakers enjoyed themselves just 100 yards away. He was woken at 6am to a breakfast of bread and margarine and a cup of black coffee. There were plenty of people who said that this was the sort of treatment needed to tame the real soccer hooligans, but many felt that the passport idea should at least be given a chance first.

In 1974, schoolboy soccer fans blamed teeny boozers for football hooliganism. Boys aged 14 or 15 were drinking up to six pints before football matches, it was claimed. These lads then started fights on the terraces or trains, which were often wrecked. The claim was made at a special get-together at a comprehensive school in Calverton, Nottinghamshire. Soccer chiefs, police and teachers met with 35 young Nottingham Forest fans to try to beat the football hooliganism menace. The claims about teeny boozing were made by two fifth formers (Year 11 pupils). Claude Richardson, head teacher of the school later said: "I was shocked by the disclosure about pre-match drinking. Boys spoke of youths of their own age drinking five to six pints, which clearly they can not take." PC John Graham added: "Only last Saturday I smelt beer on the breath of a young lad. But, when I tackled him, he told me he had been drinking his dad's home-made beer." Nottingham Forest chairman, Jim Wilmer, asked the boys to help to stamp out obscene chants and spitting, which, he said were driving away soccer fans.

In December 1975, a police inspector played the role of a football hooligan and found non-League Scarborough's anti-riot railings wanting. He climbed over spiked posts and put his hand through wire netting designed to pen in Crystal Palace fans at an FA Cup third-round tie. His verdict? "There's a lot wants doing." A Scarborough director hurriedly went off to buy 100 yards of wire netting – to add to the 300 yards of fencing that was borrowed from the local zoo – and work began immediately to strengthen the railings. League clubs were still suffering in 1976. Writing in the *Mirror*, journalist Bill Grundy said: "When Tommy Docherty, the Manchester United manager, said it was time we thought about bringing back the birch for Soccer hooligans, it's a safe bet that millions of people gave a sigh of relief and murmured: 'Thank God for common sense, at last.'" Grundy states: "Docherty made his remark at the beginning of the season, after the match with Derby County, when thugs of both sides went on the rampage. Since then, things have got worse and worse, culminating in the death of young soccer fan, Ian Pratt, on London's New Cross station."

He continued: "Culminating? What am I saying? Culminating means coming to an end. Is there the slightest sign that things are coming to an end? Not one. But there are lots of signs that worse is to come. There was a time when you could safely let your kids go to a football match on their own. But today? Well, if you don't mind them losing an eye, or having a few ribs broken, or their heads smashed in, you can still let them go alone. *And don't think that if you accompany them, you'll both come out unscathed, because there is absolutely no guarantee you will.*

"Why this should be I don't know. And the explanations I've heard don't impress me. The most common one is that kids today lead unsatisfying lives. Society offers them nothing but boredom. Like youth at all times, they crave excitement, and if life doesn't give it to them, they'll make their own after the match. Rubbish!" said Grundy, "In the dark days of the Depression life really could have been considered to be a bit empty. No telly, no transistors, no pop records or groups. No boredom at work, because few people had jobs to be bored at. Yet they went to the match on Saturday, quite often their only luxury in the week, and they behaved themselves."

Grundy goes on to state how people in the Depression were every bit as devoted to their teams as fans were in the mid-1970s. He said: "They got every bit as worked up watching their lads win or lose." The point he wanted to make though, was that – unlike the unruly fans of the 1970s – they didn't invade the pitch. They didn't fight on the terraces. They didn't spend their time after the match beating up anybody who got in their way. They didn't rampage up and down the streets around the ground, smashing windows, kicking in doors and generally going bloody mad. Grundy said: "Now, while there is no real explanation why they do behave like that these days, there are plenty of suggestions about what can be done to stop them doing it. Unfortunately, most of the suggestions seem to me to be downright daft or impracticable."

One idea that was mooted was to make offending fans report to the police station every Saturday afternoon, but Grundy felt the police had quite enough to do already without having to act as "nannies" to a bunch of thugs. He suggested these hard-core fans were fined heavily. But then decided that most wouldn't have the money, so they'd end up being sent to prison instead – and prisons were already overpopulated as it was. He stated that smaller fines wouldn't work either, because "gangs" of football hooligans would just find the money and bail their gang members out. It wouldn't really act as a deterrent. Grundy asked: "Ban them from football grounds for life?" But then what? He said: "And how do you propose to do that? By the use of 'This man is wanted' posters?" He suggested that the pensioners on the gates at football grounds – helping their clubs out – wouldn't be able to cope with a "rogues gallery".

"The more I think about it," he said, "the more I think Tommy Docherty is right. If the thugs get a thrill out of putting the boot in to some poor outnumbered opponent lying on the floor, let them see what sort of thrill they get out of being on the receiving end for a change." Grundy stated it wouldn't cost anything, it wouldn't take up any cell space and wouldn't take very long. "And, you never know, it might just work," he offered. However, he also said that violence couldn't be met with violence. "But, if you're not going to meet violence with violence, what the hell are you going to meet it with, if everything else has failed?" he continued. Meanwhile, it seemed as if the problem would only get worse and much more serious.

"One youth dead. Next week it could be two or three. Or ... how many does it have to be before we decide we've got to try something different?" he asked. "I fully understand why certain people shrink from the idea of returning to something as crude, primitive, and brutal as the birch. But, the thugs we're talking about are themselves crude, primitive and brutal," he stated. Tommy Docherty was renowned for his toughness, but it was also recognized that he was a warm, understanding and caring man. One of the things he cared about was the welfare of the vast, sensible majority of his team's supporters. He had had to live with the problem of football hooliganism in a way that most of the rest of the population did not. Grundy stated that Docherty had thought deeply about the problem. "If he now comes to the conclusion that, like it or not, this is the only way left to crack it, why shouldn't we listen to him?" Grundy concluded.

By the following year, soccer was the fastest-growing sport in the United States. There was no mystery about why it was booming across the Atlantic, while remaining in the doldrums in the UK. In America, the promoters had something to sell – an action-packed game superior to their own elephantine brand of football. Instead of offering their fans the absolute minimum – cattle-shed terraces, subterranean latrines and rubbish snack food (at the time known as "fan fare"), US footie fans were presented with the best. A family night out at an American soccer game included comfortable seats, drum majorettes, big-screen playbacks, spacious restaurants. It represented value for money. In 1977, in contrast, English football clubs were described as the "slums" of the leisure industry. Clubs had no money for investment – they just couldn't provide the attractions that would earn them money. Investors were like gold dust. Expectations were low, so, it was alleged, football matches inevitably attracted a crowd whose expectations were even lower. Commentators were confident that this is what gave rise to the football hooligans. "Raised in a concrete block, where people are treated like sheep, he passes through a concrete tunnel to a world where people are treated like pigs," wrote the *Mirror*, in September 1977. This came just after Manchester United supporters put the boot in Saint-Étienne, France. The newspaper asked: "Do United officials throw up their hands in horror at having bred fans who can't be taken anywhere? Not at all: they're simply peeved with the French for not 'segregating' the Red Army. And," wrote the *Mirror*, "that's the limit of their vision. Put the customers behind barbed wire and they're happy ..."

On 17th August 1984, after more years of hooliganism misery, it was suggested, according to a report, that a League table of soccer clubs with the most violent supporters should be started. A Government working party of 13 civil servants also wanted all League clubs to be given licences to stage matches – which could be withdrawn when there was trouble from thugs. They urged that matches between clubs at the top of the violence league – and all local Derby games – should be barred on bank holidays.

Their report also said that only members of supporters' clubs with special computerized cards should be allowed into grounds. But the group opposed the creation of a new criminal offence of football hooliganism and the withdrawal of passports from soccer thugs convicted abroad. The group also said that the sale of alcohol should not be barred inside grounds. Their report was criticized by the police and clubs alike. The Police Federation said: "Hooligans would take perverted pride in coming top of the violence league." The Football League agreed the idea was more likely to incite violence than curb it. West Ham supporter, David Crane, 22, said: "It's just what we wanted. It's like getting proper recognition." And one Newcastle United fan, Steve Ball, said: "None of these ideas will work. We know more about how to cause trouble than they know how to stop it."

In September 1985, hooliganism, "boring" football and the high cost of administration were proving a lethal combination for the UK's national sport. Dubbed "the three evils", they had driven fans away from the game far more than the tragedies of Brussels or Bradford. An exclusive *Mirror* poll showed that only 10 per cent of the first thousand of the newspaper's readers who responded to the question "Why are you staying away?" said it was because of the previous season's tragedies at the Heysel stadium and Valley Parade. Another 13 per cent said that the lack of TV exposure had caused them to lose interest. Hundreds of readers went beyond the pool, instigated by *Mirror Sport*, and wrote detailed letters explaining why they thought a further one-and-a-half million were projected to desert the game in the 1985/6 season. The voting showed:

Hooliganism	27%
Boring football	25%
Cost	25%
No TV soccer	13%
Tragedies	10%

Readers attacked overpaid footballers, who were no longer giving them value for money, and overpaid managers, including Sunderland's Lawrie McMenemy, who, they said, was "guilty of outlandish after-match comments" and "forever projecting their images". Many readers called for a Super League to bring higher-quality games, and a change in the offside law to encourage more attacking play. Margaret Thatcher said she planned to review her Government's anti-hooliganism measures after the first six weeks of the season (1985/6). At this point, many hooligans were staying away from matches. Some even wrote to the newspaper to tell them why: "Not enough hooliganism." An anonymous member of the infamous ICF (Inter City Firm) wrote: "We are keeping away from football because of the new stupid laws against hooliganism. We don't bother innocent people, just the 'Firm' of other teams that come down for trouble." However, the writer added ominously: "PS, We will be back soon." It was taken as a clear warning to clubs and police not to become complacent in their efforts to keep the season free from trouble.

Sure enough, the trouble was far from over. In November 1987, the *Mirror* asked: "How can the Football Association be so stupid as to go for a sponsor whose product isn't allowed in soccer grounds?" While a father grieved for his son who died because of a kicking by drunken soccer thugs, the FA admitted that the FA Cup was about to be named after a beer. The Cup is the most historic soccer trophy in the world. It has always been given a respect and a tradition that nothing else in the game could match. The newspaper argued that there was nothing wrong with sponsorship. Without it many grounds would have closed, many sports might even have collapsed, but, said the article: "… there are sponsorships and sponsorships". The paper said: "It is inconceivable that the Cup and the England team should be handed over lock, stock and beer barrel. The FA knows, as well as anybody, that it is too much drink that causes most of the violence, the injuries and the deaths at grounds, in the streets near them and on the trains and coaches going to them.

"And that those hooligans who shamed Britain abroad – and had us banned from Europe – were full of it. That is what the army of England fans who will go to West Germany next year for the European Cup Championships have already been warned against. The FA is the guardian as well as the governing body of soccer. Unfortunately, it is full of old dodderers who seem to have taken leave of their senses."

The *Mirror* was praised in the House of Commons the following day for exposing the controversial £12million deal the football bosses had struck with a brewery company over the FA Cup. Labour MP Roland Boyes attacked the sponsorship deal because of the link between alcohol and football hooliganism. The FA Cup – after 115 years – was set to be renamed the FFA Cup due to the deal with Foster's Lager. Boyes blasted the FA and said: "It was an absolutely ludicrous decision to sell off the most famous competition in the world to a brewery. It is especially unacceptable when one of the major causes of football hooliganism is drunken slobs with no interest in the game whatsoever. These hooligan fans were the cause of English clubs being banned from European competitions." The row became so intense that health experts warned that watching Cup ties could seriously damage health, and they worried over the possible adverse influence of the lager brand. The three-year deal was viewed with "considerable dismay" by the Health Education Authority. In a statement the authority said: "Further strengthening of the association between sport and alcohol has serious implications for the issue of alcohol abuse in general, young people's drinking in particular and the role of alcohol in the violence which disfigures much of football." However, the Football Association was determined to go ahead with the sponsorship.

Things changed, however, in January 1988, when it was announced that the FA Cup was to stay the FA Cup. The Football Association retreated from its decision to allow the sponsorship by the brewery. The *Mirror* claimed a victory – with the help of its readers – in sporting history.

Progress did happen, but it was slow. In August 1998, football hooliganism had fallen for the fourth year in a row, with arrests falling 10 per cent in the previous season. Only 3,437 fans were arrested in the four English leagues, according to National Criminal Intelligence Service data. And, in the FA, Coca Cola and Auto Windscreen Cups there were 897 arrests – down 29 per cent. Police picked up 1,148 people in Euro 96. Home Office Minister

David Maclean announced: "The popularity of the game is rising while hooliganism is diminishing."

However, the trouble was still evident in 2003 when David Beckham admitted that England might have to lock out "racist fans" and play in an empty stadium. The then squad skipper said: "It's a shame. But if it's going to end the trouble that goes on, then we should consider it." UEFA were rumoured to be thinking about ordering England to play their June match against Slovakia without a crowd after racist taunts and rioting by home fans at the April match, where the team beat Turkey. The Slovakian FA had been fined £27,000 for their fans' racism during a match against England in 2002. Former England star Terry McDermott said: "Beckham's right. But it's tough for the real fans." Beckham acknowledged that locking crowds out of international matches would be: "sad for football and for its fans", but that there might be no choice. He admitted that the harsh move might be the only way to stamp out the racist thugs who were blighting the game. His views were echoed by the then current and former players who praised him for speaking out against hooligans. Beckham – at the time a Manchester United star – said: "If we had to play a qualifying game behind closed doors it would be sad for proper England fans who would suffer because of the small minority of people that are doing this. It's a shame for young kids who are coming to watch players they admire. But, if it's going to put an end to the trouble that goes on, then we should consider it. I can't imagine a game where there's no crowd. It shouldn't happen, but it might have to." He spoke out in the wake of a pitch invasion and racist taunts by England fans at the club's European Championship against Turkey in Sunderland. He said: "It is disappointing when you see the trouble that goes on around football matches. Of course players notice it and worry about it. We've friends and family in the stands. There was a period when most of it had stopped but it seems to be creeping back in."

If UEFA had decided England did have to play "behind closed doors", it would have been a blow to the cash-strapped FA, which had had to lay off staff due to financial problems. UEFA had already fined the FA £9,000 for trouble caused by visiting supporters. Tottenham striker and former England star, Les Ferdinand, said it would "be a shame for football in general" if the Slovakia game was played in an empty arena. He added: "I was surprised more wasn't done to prevent the trouble at Sunderland, especially given the history between the two sets of fans. The level of hooliganism is certainly less than when I started my career and it's a shame the problem has reared its head again." Ex-England international Chris Waddle said: "We have got to start selecting grounds where there is no chance of the fans being able to get on to the pitch. I understand what David Beckham is saying, but as a player you like to see England fans in the ground. Other teams do not relish coming over here when they have to face the England supporters." Meanwhile, McDermott added: "Beckham has hit the nail on the head. The hooligan problem is probably as bad now as it was 20 or 30 years ago. It worries me when you see fans invading the pitch. It just takes one nutter with a knife to stab a player. If playing behind closed doors is the only way to stop it, it should be considered." Ex-Northern Ireland manager Lawrie McMenemy said: "Full marks to David for standing up and being counted. Playing behind closed doors is the ultimate punishment." However, one-time manager of Wales, Terry Yorath, disagreed, and said that locking out the crowd would mean the racists had won. He said he'd witnessed closed stands abroad and it didn't solve anything. "These people have got to be pointed out, picked out and cleared out," he stated. In Sunderland, yobs tried to attack coaches carrying Turkish fans and chanted racist abuse at them inside the arena. It led to clashes with riot police on the streets.

In 2007, a radio show aired the views of one of its listeners who phoned in to express their opinion – that the reason there was no violence at football matches was because the "poor" people could no longer afford to go to games. This came from an Italian supporter who the *Mirror* described as: "exploring excuses for the murderous hooliganism that is destroying the game in his country". The Italian's assumption, wrote the newspaper, was that ever since ticket prices spiraled out of reach of the common man in England, thuggery had become a thing of the past. It said: "This Fever Pitch generation of football fans doesn't understand the tribalism of English football. New football supporters don't want to understand it. It scares them. They know that it's cool to pretend to be obsessive about the game, buy their £50 replica kit every couple of years and get 'Rooney' or 'Henry' printed on the back, but they don't really want to burrow too deep into its culture. And, they certainly don't want to countenance the idea they're part of anything as crude as group aggression." The paper stated that the inevitable corollary of this argument was that if cash-rich Premiership clubs, swimming in a nectar sea of "television moolah", did the right thing and slashed ticket prices then the thugs would be back. It argued: "And that's where the argument gets dangerous. And, frankly unpleasant. Because to equate wealth with good behaviour is about as bankrupt as an argument can get. There are reasons why people are dying at Italian football matches and not at English ones and they have nothing to do with exiling the working classes from our stadia." The article continued: "We did something about our hooligan problems, for a start, whereas the Italians and the Spanish appeased by UEFA and FIFA, did nothing." English clubs, by this time, had implemented the Taylor Report. With Government help, they used banning orders to keep grounds free of known hooligans. The clubs made huge strides in striking at core issues in the hooligan culture, most noticeably racism and consumption of alcohol in view of the pitch. Many of the clubs were justifiably proud of the anti-racism work they promoted in their communities. They deserved recognition for their initiatives, and Arsenal and Wolves were highly praised. However, elsewhere in Europe the leniency continued. When Paolo di Canio made a habit of making Fascist salutes when he returned to Italy to play with Lazio in 2005, he was fined 10,000 euros and banned for one game. When Spanish fans abused England's black players in November 2004, the Spanish Football Federation was fined £44,000. In the middle of the first decade of the 21st century, racist abuse in Spain and Italy was routine. It was common to see missiles thrown on the pitch. In England, however, that kind of behaviour was now viewed as a major incident. English football had the chance to bring its ticket prices down and welcome back the true fans it had had to leave behind.

There was uproar in June 2010 when angry relatives of Hillsborough victims slated the Tory sports minister, Jeremy Hunt, after he blamed fans for the disaster. The blundering culture secretary was branded "an ignorant disgrace" following his crass remarks over the 1989 tragedy, which left 96 Liverpool supporters dead. He was later forced to issue a grovelling apology for comments he had made in a TV interview. Hunt was praising the behaviour of England World Cup fans in South Africa when he blurted out: "I mean, not a single arrest for a football-related offence, and the terrible problems that we had in Heysel and Hillsborough in the 1980s seem now to be behind us." His words sparked outrage in Merseyside – especially after a 1990 official inquiry led by the late Lord Justice Taylor found that police crowd control was the main cause of the horrific crush at the Sheffield Wednesday stadium. In an attempt to limit the damage, Hunt issued a statement saying: "I know that fan unrest played no part in the terrible events of April 1989. I apologize to Liverpool fans and the families of those killed and injured if my comments caused any offence." However, Margaret Aspinall, chair of the Hillsborough Family Support Group, said his apology was too late. She said: "I am fed up of people saying things like that. For 21 years we have been fighting for justice, to get the message out that it was not down to drink or hooliganism. He is the Culture Secretary, he should know better. I want him to understand that he has re-opened old wounds which should have healed many years ago." Labour MP Derek Twigg told the Commons: "This is a disgrace. I've spoken to some of the families who lost loved ones at Hillsborough – and they're deeply distressed and angry." Labour leadership contender, Andy Burnham, who led a campaign to release confidential Hillsborough documents, added: "It's depressing to hear a Cabinet minister make this remark. It shows a casual ignorance about one of the biggest man-made disasters this country has ever seen."

But football hooliganism did seem to be on the rise once again in 2010, when it was reported that "a fresh crop of yobs – some aged only 13 – is plaguing football". Violence around matches involving hooligan teenagers had almost trebled in the three years leading up to 2010. Police feared the "teeny boot boys" would be a curse on the game for generations to come. The problem was highlighted in figures obtained by BBC's 5 *Live Breakfast* from the Association of Chief Police Officers. In 2007, police recorded 38 clashes near stadiums or on public transport, where some rival fans involved were under 20. In the 2009/10 season, the figure was 103 – 44 per cent of all hooligan incidents, up from 33 per cent three years before. ACPO football investigations chief, Andy Holt, said: "We're going to be stuck with this sort of behaviour potentially for some while, so it's something we're acutely aware of. People are engaging in football disorder who perhaps weren't around in the heyday of football violence 15 to 20 years ago. This is an extremely worrying trend and one we are acutely aware of." Overall, in 2010, disorder incidents had risen from 114 in 2007 to 221 in the 2009/10 season. Two-thirds of those banned were aged between 20 and 30, but a 13-year-old was slapped with a three-year ban in October 2009. The eldest person to receive an order was 71. In September 2010, British Transport Police appealed for information about young hooligans who forced a woman off a train and onto the railway tracks after Cardiff City played Millwall.

Hillsborough was back in the news in March 2012, when shocking claims came to light. Margaret Thatcher, the prime minister in 1989, had been told by a senior Merseyside police officer that "drunken Liverpool fans" caused the Hillsborough disaster. The revelation, which rightly outraged Hillsborough campaigners, was discovered in leaked Government documents, which included Cabinet minutes and letters to and from No. 10. The papers showed that a secret briefing involving Chief Constable Sir Kenneth Oxford and other top officers was held four days after the 15th April tragedy in 1989. The PM was then told: "One officer, born and bred in Liverpool, said he was deeply ashamed to say that it was drunken Liverpool fans who had caused this disaster – just as they caused the deaths at Heysel." A note on the letter, marked "confidential", was initialed "MT" and the words, "drunken Liverpool fans", were underlined. In the letter, sent just days after Thatcher visited the scene of the tragedy, Sir Kenneth added: "A key factor in causing the disaster was the fact that large numbers of Liverpool fans had turned up without tickets. This was getting lost sight of in attempts to blame the police, the football authorities, etc." Oxford, who died in 1998, was also angry with how the disaster was reported and "uneasy" about the way Liverpool's ground was being "turned into a shrine". Margaret Aspinall, whose 18-year-old son James died in the crush said: "I find it appalling and a disgrace. I can't believe the Chief Constable made remarks about Anfield being made a shrine – 96 lives were lost. The fans needed somewhere to pay their respects."

The Hillsborough Justice Campaign said: "We are really concerned that the emphasis is totally on Merseyside Police here and not on South Yorkshire Police." An official report by Lord Justice Taylor blamed the FA Cup semi-final tragedy on the South Yorkshire Police. The leaked documents were being examined by the Hillsborough Independent Panel. But the *Mirror* stated that it was a small wonder the truth never got out about Hillsborough. So desperate was the desire to blame drunken, ticketless fans, even top Merseyside cops joined the cover-up. Lord Justice Taylor had dismissed those factors, blaming South Yorkshire Police bungling for the 96 deaths. But, before his report got out, that force leaned on Tory MPs, the media and their own top people to shift the guilt. It was no surprise that Oxford backed the party line. He had blamed the Toxteth riots entirely on "black hooligans", ignoring his heavy-handed policing as a factor. It was also no surprise that Thatcher was given a report from an "unnamed senior officer" that drunken fans were to blame. No one told her of the Merseyside Police Federation secretary's calls from cops at the game urging him to "redress the balance". "And, it was no surprise that the Tories wanted to use the disaster to bring in their vindictive Football Supporters Bill as a stick to beat every fan in the land," said the newspapers.

In September 2012, the *Mirror* used a 300-year-old quote from Edmund Burke: "All that is necessary for the triumph of evil is that good men do nothing." In an article, the newspaper condemned the way in which the Hillsborough tragedy had been handled. When the verdict of the Hillsborough Independent Panel was released, the newspaper said: "For years, decades, we have all stood silent – at

best – as our ears have been assailed by the football politics of hate."
It cited the chants that suggested Arsène Wenger was a paedophile,
it cited the hisses to replicate the sound of the gas chambers and
the suggestions that Emmanuel Adebayor deserved to be a victim
of the Togo bus tragedy and not a survivor. The article continued:
"[we are all …] guilty of allowing it to fester, to infect and shame the
game. Guilty of turning a blind eye to what was happening in front of
our faces. Guilty of willfully ignoring what was crystal clear, because
to admit it was just too damned inconvenient … the bitter truth is
that far too many of us, good men, have done nothing, absolutely
nothing." It stated: "It is not freedom of expression, as some claim. It
is sick, evidence of a world where all normal moral values have gone
into abeyance. And, it is time, long beyond time, for it to end. Now."

Hillsborough happened because of a "failure in police control",
not because drunken fans were behaving like hooligans. And there
was then a huge police cover-up. The *Mirror* said that the "political
hatred" in the grounds of all clubs must stop. It was time to take a
stand, as "the time has come … for the good people, all of us, to
stand up". It concluded its article on prejudice by saying we are: "A
nation that must no longer do nothing." In hooliganism today, some
gangs of thugs share characteristics, including links to far-right and
racist organizations. The Heysel disaster in 1985 occurred when
a "charge" by Liverpool fans at Juventus supporters caused a wall
to collapse, resulting in 39 deaths. It was to prove a watershed
in the history of English football hooliganism. The following year,
the Public Order Act 1986 permitted courts to ban supporters from
grounds. The Football Spectators Act in 1989 allowed the banning

of convicted hooligans from international matches (where most of the trouble is today). The Football (Disorder) Act 1999 changed the discretionary power of the courts to keep order to a duty, while the Football Disorder Act 2000 abolished the distinction between domestic and international bans. The Football Offences Act 1991 created specific offences, such as throwing missiles onto pitches and participating in racist or indecent chanting. It also made it an offence to go onto the pitch without lawful authority. In March 2012, Scotland implemented two new offences in the Offensive Behaviour at Football and Threatening Communications (Scotland) Act 2012 in order to overcome the increasing problem with regard to threatening behaviour (particularly related to inciting religious hatred).

Today alcohol appears to have little effect on "new" football violence. In the past, it was clear that many hooligans were drunk, but great measures have been taken in recent years to prevent fans from becoming incapacitated while attending matches. There are those that believe that the media has had a huge part to play in inciting fans prior to matches, with explosive headlines and grabbing articles full of aggressive and combative language. Banning orders are now on the decrease – it's been proved they work. Police estimate that more than 90 per cent of those whose banning orders expired in the early part of the 21st century no longer pose the risk of football hooliganism, or disorders as they are now more commonly referred to. However, it remains to be seen how today's teenagers behave. This book takes a look at some of the wilder cases of hooliganism that have blighted the history of football over the past 100 years.

1906 – Sheffield Football Riot

A meeting was held by the FA in Sheffield on 14th February 1906 to look into a disturbance that occurred at the Owlerton ground after a League match between Sheffield Wednesday and Preston North End. It took nearly five hours and included directors, players, spectators and police. "There was an unseemly disturbance in the vicinity of the dressing room after the match, and actual molestation of the Preston North End players in the journey from the ground to the hotel, missiles having been thrown and offensive conduct indulged in. Evidence proves that the offenders were persons who had been spectators at the match."

The meeting delved into the causes for the disturbance and found:

1. "The match was not played in a proper spirit, the conduct indulged in by both teams being calculated to bring discredit upon the game.

2. "The match was not properly controlled by the referee, and there was a want of alertness on the part of the linesman.

3. "Mr. T Houghton, a director of the Preston North End club, conducted himself very improperly towards the spectators in the neighbourhood of the dressing room at the close of the match.

4. "The players of the Preston North End club conducted themselves in a vulgar manner at the dressing room window at the close of the match."

As a result the following measures were taken. Both teams were censured, the referee Mr J W Bailey, from Leicester, and the linesmen, Rhodes and North, were also censured. Houghton was suspended from football management for one month from 26th February 1906. It was decided that it was impossible to pinpoint exactly who the perpetrators were in the crowd, so each and every fan was fined £1, which had to be paid by 26th February. The meeting also declared that the directors of the Sheffield Wednesday club had done all that they could to ensure the proper conduct of the match, but that the spectators should be taught that such behaviour could not be tolerated. The Owlerton ground was consequently closed for 14 days from the same date.

1909 – Angry Scenes at Football Riot in Glasgow

As a protest against the fact that no extra-time was played after a second drawn game in the Scottish Cup final in Glasgow between Celtic and Rangers – in the belief that the drawn games were prearranged in order to multiply "gate money" – a proportion of the crowd at Hampden Park on 17th April 1909 caused a riot that resulted in more than 50 people being injured, including a number of policemen. Some of the rioters smashed the barricades, made a huge bonfire with them, and then set pay boxes alight at the entrance of the field.

It was one of the most serious football riots on record. The damage amounted to around £1,000. About 60,000 had gathered at the grounds to witness the Scottish Cup final between Celtic and Rangers, as the match between the teams had resulted in a draw the previous week. When the second-round match drew to an end and the scores were again 1-1, the crowd grew restless and disorderly and there were shouts of: "Play on!"

However, there were no arrangements in place – no plan had been mapped out by the authorities and the players were allowed to retire from the field. This was the signal for the outbreak of the rioting. A few hundred men and youths jumped the barricades and invaded the pitch, where they were soon followed by thousands of others. The police numbers were relatively small, but they did try to resist the onward rush of the crowd. The situation became so threatening that mounted police were ordered to enter the enclosure. However, this just incensed the mob, and stones and bottles were thrown, the goalposts were torn up and broken, and the nets destroyed. A gang of youths seized the roller and did considerable damage to the pitch. Several times, mounted police charged the crowd, but they were met with a shower of missiles. The police were effectively powerless. To add to the seriousness of the situation, a number of rioters broke up the barricades and set fire to them. The huge bonfire covered track and turf, but this didn't stop the rioters, who then "seized" the pay boxes and added them to the flames, which created a massive and alarming blaze. The fire brigade was called, but, for more than half an hour, they were unable to get to the blaze. The mob stopped the firemen from entering the ground and, as a consequence, were doused by hoses being turned on them. The rioters then rushed at the firefighters, throwing missiles before taking charge of the hoses, which they jumped on before cutting in several places.

Meanwhile, the large crowd was swaying and rushing about to escape being trampled on by police and horses. Fears grew for the safety of the pavilion and the grandstands, but the police succeeded in keeping the crowd at the opposite end of the field. The flames from the pay boxes alarmed residents living in the vicinity of the ground – many of whom fled from their homes screaming. Eventually extra police were drafted in from the city and the field was gradually cleared of spectators. Ambulances were called and the injured sent to local infirmaries – where most were just suffering from cuts and bruises. The police suffered a number of casualties – many had head, facial and back wounds, some fairly serious. After this event, football officials considered withholding the Cup for the season as a punishment to all concerned. A meeting was held on 19th April 1909 by the Scottish Football Association in Glasgow where it *was* decided to withhold the Cup for the year as a sign of disapproval for the riot. Two days after the affray between Celtic and Rangers, five people were reported to be in a serious condition in hospital. One rioter was fined £5 for assaulting the police, while two other men were remanded in custody for causing injury with pieces of iron and severing pieces of hosepipe.

1912 – Irish Football Riot: Spectators Rush the Field

On 21st May 1912, the *Londonderry Sentinel* described how Irish football was also suffering from rioting by spectators. In the North-West Irish Charity Cup, when two players fell, and other players went to help them, it prompted large numbers of the crowd to come rushing onto the pitch. Despite the efforts of the committee of the Derry Guilds Club, aided by the police, all the Derry Institute players were attacked by the crowd. The referee, James Andrews, and one of the linesmen, Holland, were also assaulted, while the ground's caretaker, Mr Tolard, was struck in the eye with a stone. The Institute players eventually got to the pavilion, but the crowd took up a threatening attitude and endeavoured to rush the pavilion. Luckily, extra police arrived and the crowd was forced outside the ground.

1958 – City Seeks Control of Pitches: Action against Soccer Rowdies

A sensational move was made in December 1958 to end the soccer "rowdyism" that was rocking a city. In Glasgow, clashes between supporters of the two leading clubs, Celtic and Rangers, had forced the City magistrates to call for help from the Government. They had decided to ask the Secretary of State for Scotland, John Maclay, to give them unique powers to license the city's soccer grounds so that they could enforce rules to control the behaviour of crowds. "And the big question being asked in Glasgow now is: Could it lead to licences being withdrawn and grounds closed if the fans continued to misbehave?" asked newspapers. Baillie O'Sullivan, one of the magistrates, said the move had been made to safeguard Glasgow's reputation.

It followed an approach to Rangers FC, Celtic FC, the Scottish Football Association and the Scottish Football League. The magistrates sent their recommendations for dealing with hooliganism but: "Rangers and the SFL have not replied," said O'Sullivan. "We don't know what their attitude is. We think the suggestions we made are reasonable and necessary to end the trouble." The magistrates asked for a ban on banners and flags at matches, for a separate boys' enclosure and for a limit on the gate at the Celtic/Rangers games. Celtic disagreed with the idea of a boys' enclosure and the Scottish Football Association rejected a gate limit. There was also a great deal of trouble at English grounds during the 1958/9 season, and the Football League had already ordered certain clubs to post warning notices against bad behaviour. But, in Scotland, Football League secretary, Alan Hardaker, said he couldn't visualize any city administration south of the Borders wanting powers to control grounds.

1959 – Arsenal-Colchester Cup Match

A mob of football fans who were locked out of the Arsenal–Colchester match on 28th January 1959, because a London Underground hold-up made them late, stormed a block of flats overlooking Arsenal's ground in an attempt to see the game. Nearly 500 fans were held up on their way to the Highbury replay, when a signal fault brought chaos to the Piccadilly Line Tube service. When the fans reached the ground and found the gates were shut, they made for nearby Aubert Court, a six-storey block of Islington borough council flats in Avenell Road, Highbury. As the football crowd streamed in on the ground floor, people living in the flats fought their way out to get to the police. When the police, including some on horseback, arrived at the flats, some of the football fans had smashed doors to get out onto the roof. One tenant, Violet Hill, said: "It was bedlam. The crowd were ringing all the flat doorbells and asking if they could watch the game from the balconies. I believe they broke down the door on to the roof. There must have been 300 people in our part of the building alone. A mounted policeman turned some of them away when they tried to break iron gates to get on the roof of maisonettes nearby." Mrs Hill continued, "We've had this sort of trouble before, but this is the worst I have seen." A neighbour, Minnie Harris, said: "The fans were trampling up and down the stairs for about an hour."

One of the fans who was shut out of the ground said last

night: "If the Tube trains hadn't been late, this would never have happened. My trip should have taken fifteen minutes. It took seventy-five minutes. I had a 12s. 6d ticket for the match, but the gates were closed when I finally got there because the ground was full." The Underground chaos also hit many of the 62,686 fans who did get into the Highbury ground to see Arsenal win 4-0. During the game, loudspeaker appeals were made to the crowd, asking those who had come by Tube to go home some other way. A London Transport spokesman said: "The failure arose as a result of damage to signal equipment in a tunnel. Owing to the breakdown, trains were taking up to ninety minutes – instead of the normal ten minutes or so – from Central London to the Arsenal station." The spokesman added: "We very much regret the delay to trains."

1964 – Busby Team Quits Train to Take the Coach

On 5th January 1964, 500 screaming, shouting football fans stopped a Cup-tie "special" train. Cup holders Manchester United were led from the train by manager, Matt Busby, to finish the journey home by coach. Railway workers fought an hour-long battle to move the train out of Snow Hill station, Birmingham. But Cup-crazy United fans pulled the communication cord nearly 50 times. The train arrived at Manchester's Piccadilly station more than four hours late – and British Railways ordered a top-level investigation into the "Battle of Snow Hill".

United had beaten Southampton 3-2 in the third round of the Cup after being two goals down. Later, as the night train travelled back to Manchester, the trouble started. A relief engine was sent out at Banbury, Oxfordshire, because of a suspected brake fault. But the reason the brakes were not working was because fans were pulling the communication cord. At Bordesley station, Birmingham, the "special" was delayed another hour because the brakes were locked. With another engine towing, the train travelled the rest of the way into Snow Hill, still with the brakes jammed on. There, railway police reinforcements – with a dog – were called from New Street station to help the police at Snow Hill. As fast as engineers went down the 11-coach train freeing the brakes, fans pulled the communication cord and locked them again. Work on the station was almost at a standstill as shouting, screaming United fans roamed the platforms.

A railway spokesman said: "Snow Hill was the climax of the battle. It was a near-riot. The restaurant car had to be closed because of the general uproar by the jubilant supporters. But, there was no damage to the train. The team left the train at Wolverhampton because of the fans."

United inside-left, David Herd, said: "We were tired of all the stopping. The boss pulled us off the train and we got home by coach – four hours late." There was no more trouble after Wolverhampton. However, police were called twice to a "special" train taking Manchester City fans home from Swindon, Wiltshire, where City lost 2-1. A railway spokesman in Manchester said: "These incidents must make us think seriously whether we can continue with football excursions from Manchester."

In April 1964, one way suggested to stop soccer "rowdies" was to introduce high wire fences. It would mean the possibility of closing grounds for a time, but it was thought it would curb hooliganism. One journalist thought that the treatment of players who behaved badly – being sent off and fined, and eventually suspended if necessary – should be applied to fans who disrupted the enjoyment of the game, or those who posed a danger to other spectators. It was suggested that magistrates should apply the same sanctions as those given to "rogue" players. The journalist also suggested that huge fines be introduced. And he felt that imprisonment might be the answer – or a compulsory order report each Saturday at a police station. He further felt useful work could be allocated on Saturdays to the soccer louts. He said: "It seems tragic that the man [on the terraces] should be penalized because the very few behave like wild animals."

About 25,000 football fans rioted and set fire to a stadium in Athens, in Greece, on 17th June 1964. Police said the fans were incensed because they thought the match – a Cup semi-final – had been "fixed". Spectators tore down fences, surged across the pitch and broke into the club premises. There they set furniture alight and smashed windows, chanting: "Peru! Peru!"

This was a reference to the Lima disaster the previous month when 301 people died in a riot at a match between Peru and Argentina. The match in Greece was between the country's top teams – Panathinaikos from Athens and Olympiacos of Piraeus. It ended in a 1-1 draw. Club-swinging police battled with the fans and finally drove them from the stadium. Two months later, in an unrelated incident, soccer fans found themselves "on trial".

Train-wrecking football fans got a "last-chance" warning from British Railways on 12th August 1964, when they were told by a BR spokesman that they could have their soccer "specials" back for a trial period at the start of the coming season – even though hooligans had caused thousands of pounds of damage to carriages in 1963 – but that: "At the first sign of wanton damage the trains will be withdrawn immediately." The warning was given to fans of League Champions Liverpool and Everton, the "Mersey millionaires", by James Trainor, railway district manager at Liverpool. Vandals were so destructive in the previous year that the "specials" were taken off during the season. Trainor said: "If we get the same treatment during the trial – from August 22 to October 3 – we shall withdraw the 'specials' at once. We have to protect the travelling public." He also said that the football trains would be limited to two for each match. Only corridor trains would be used. At least two transport policemen would travel on each "special". There would be no stops on the way from Liverpool to the matches. But trains would call at suburban stations on the return. Trainor said: "Communication cords were pulled dozens of times last year by fans who wanted a train to stop at unscheduled stations. We hope our new arrangements will end this trouble." BR's new tough line followed weeks of talks with football club officials from Liverpool and Everton.

Then, in November 1964, the next move to beat the soccer "rowdies" was unveiled. It was announced that train marshals would be introduced as the latest move to stamp out soccer crowd hooliganism on trips to and from matches. The idea came from Wales. Alan Rowcliffe, secretary of the Welsh area of the National Federation of Supporters' Clubs, said: "Starting this weekend – when Cardiff travel to London for the Second Division match at Crystal Palace – we shall have official stewards or marshals looking after every carriage to make sure no damage is done. If anyone is seen to take toilet rolls to throw on to the pitch we want him stopped before he gets to the match. If they pull out light bulbs, break windows or pull communication cords on the trip home, we want the offenders identified. We have got to clear our name, and don't want any more soccer specials stopped. And the train marshals who will watch over every carriage can do the job."

Tony Pullein, national secretary of the supporters' clubs agreed: "We support this Welsh plan and are recommending it to all the English Supporters' clubs as well. In particular we shall emphasize it to the people who follow teams where trouble usually occurs. We hope they will see this is a real way to overcome the trouble. Then, perhaps no more soccer excursions would be banned – as they were in Liverpool last year and Stoke this season – because of the bad behaviour of a few."

It was suggested that tough measures were the only way to beat "the toughs". The train marshals were seen as a positive first step.

1965 – British Sports Appalled by Barbaric Behaviour of Rome

In October 1965, British sportsmen were appalled by the barbaric behaviour of Rome football fans at the Roma–Chelsea game in the Italian capital. Minister of sport, Denis Howell, was moved to say that Chelsea's conduct and composure reflected great credit upon British sport. But, before British sportsmen could get all "self-righteous about hot-blooded continentals," stated the *Mirror*, "let them consider how cold-blooded British Soccer fans behaved at their previous weekend matches." There was a riot at the Manchester United–Liverpool game.

Club windows were smashed by Merseyside hooligans after Liverpool lost. Directors and guests had to scatter to avoid being hurt. Missiles were hurled on the field at Huddersfield, fighting broke out among the fans and the police had to move in. Police had to intervene, too, at Ipswich and Burnley, where one youth was carried away on a stretcher. "Sure. Rome was very nasty by all accounts," wrote the *Mirror* journalist, "but some of our British football fans are nothing to write home about either." The only good thing that could be said was that in 1965, thugs and hooligans were in the minority. However, as the paper points out, "they have been ruining football for some time". These were the same "louts" who smashed up railway coaches by ripping up upholstery and sickening everyone with their "filthy" behaviour. It was mooted that it was time the football clubs got really tough, and that the vast majority of decent football supporters united to squash the hooligans before they could start making trouble. The *Mirror* said: "If we're not careful, there will soon be a new version of the old saying: When in Rome, don't do as the Liverpudlians do."

1967 – "Let's Birch the Soccer Rowdies"

"Bring back the birch ..." is what the newspapers cried out in May 1967. They were citing the suggestion by a League official in response to the ongoing football hooliganism at grounds all over the British Isles. The League and Football Association had already started looking into the problem of the terrace "rowdies," noted the official, who said: "I think the next step will be to ask the Government for stronger penalties for thugs. Personally, I would like to see any fans caught fighting punished by birching ..."

The suggestions kept coming. In September 1967, a soccer boss was fielding a new "team" to beat the threat of hooliganism. It involved 12 miniskirted models. Their job? Well, they had to parade around the Second Division Birmingham City's ground during the half-time interval: the theory was that fans would start wolf-whistling rather than wanting to throw bottles and start fights. The plan was devised and unveiled by Birmingham's administrative manager, David Exall, who said: "Much of the rowdy business is caused by boredom. But what red-blooded chap could possibly be bored with so much leg about? Maybe leg shows at soccer grounds all over the country could save the Minister of Sport and his psychiatrists a bit of bother."

The girls and their miniskirts would be provided by a Birmingham boutique called *Fanny's*. Exall said: "We don't have trouble with hooligans here. That's mainly because we put on displays at half-time – things like Judo. Now we are going to try the mini-skirt models. It should also keep the girl fans happy – fashion and football combined." The manager of *Fanny's*, 19-year-old Pat Mellor, said: "We're hoping the minis will be a big hit. They should certainly draw a few more whistles than the referee …"

1971 – More calls to "Bring back the Birch" for Soccer Hooligans

A campaign to bring back the birch for soccer thugs got underway on 2nd August 1971. Birmingham councillor George Griffiths wrote to FA chairman Dr Andrew Stephen, giving details of his plan. He intended to ask his city council to support the campaign. He said: "I am deadly serious. These young thugs must be stopped before some innocent person gets killed. I know that the subject of birching always causes controversy – I think it is the only real answer." Another call for stiffer penalties for soccer "rowdies" was made by a magistrate in Halifax, where hundreds of fans terrorized shoppers and traders before the Watney Cup match with Manchester United. The magistrate, Fred Hargreaves, cited the Isle of Man – where young offenders could still be birched – as an example of how hooliganism could be controlled. He sent an 18-year-old youth to a detention centre for three months for assaulting a police officer and using threatening behaviour.

1972 – Soccer Fans Riot in Streets

A battle was fought through the streets of Barcelona on 24th May 1972 between thousands of Glasgow Rangers football fans and Spanish police. Cars were smashed, shop windows were pushed in – and the injured were left lying where they fell. The trouble started inside the local stadium – where Rangers won the European Cup Winners' Cup by beating Moscow Dynamo – then continued in the streets with a vengeance. The Scottish fans clashed with hundreds of Spaniards, and the police soon lost control of the situation. At one luxury hotel a massive plant was ripped out of a decorative pot by Rangers fans and dumped on top of a parked car, extensively damaging the roof of the vehicle. As fighting moved from street to street, beer cans were lobbed through shop windows, and the injured lay in large numbers on the ground. Many police were also reported to be injured. Reinforcements were rushed to the airport to protect it from the fans streaming there to catch their charter flights. The rioting crowd marred Rangers' triumph. Just minutes after Rangers won, the battle between khaki-uniformed police and the red, white and blue bedecked Scottish fans began. Fans spilled onto the pitch to acclaim and chair their heroes. For three minutes, the police tolerated the incredible overspill, which plunged the once-green pitch into a mass of colour and near-hysteria. Then it all started. The batons came out and the crowd retreated towards the perimeter, leaving the bodies of the battered and beaten behind them. It was a frightening scene, which didn't end there.

The crowd came back like a marauding army, according to eyewitness accounts, and the police retreated in a hurry. The whole stadium was at war. The police and the fire brigade were under fire from all sides, as flying fists and cushions were showered on them. But they regrouped, and in time, after a quarter of an hour of infighting, the battle was confined to a few isolated outbreaks. The police might not have been to blame initially – wrote a reporter, Bob Russell, in the *Mirror* – but some of the brutality that he witnessed, including the police "hacking" at supporters with their batons and kicking them with their uniform boots (especially the already injured lying on the floor) was sickening, he said. Almost an hour after the finish the ugly mood was still prominent. Wooden seats were shattered and pieces showered down in the direction of the blitzed police. Then came the worst moment. Bottles with their necks broken cascaded onto the cinder track in the direction of officials and overworked ambulance crews. Ironically, Rangers had beaten Moscow Dynamo in a show worthy of champions. Left-winger Willie Johnston was the hero, nailing the Russians with two crisply taken goals in the 40th and 51st minutes. Earlier, centre-forward Colin Stein put Rangers on the road to success with a 24-minute goal. Dynamo's goals – which came after Rangers had built a 3-0 lead – were scored by Vladimir Eschtrekov and Aleksandr Makhovikov. However, after the match, Dynamo lodged an official protest, alleging that their players were terrified by "completely drunk" Scottish fans.

Meanwhile, back in the UK, magistrates started their own "get tough" campaign with the first soccer "rowdies" of the 1972/3 season, when they made it clear that they would be just as severe with spectators as referees were with players. In Leicester, two teenage fans were fined £150 each for carrying offensive weapons at the First Division match with Arsenal. One had a brick and the other a length of piping. Another three teenagers were each fined £100 for threatening behaviour. Ten more fans were bound over for £100 each, while the court heard about 40 Arsenal supporters who had rushed onto the pitch during the game. Leicester magistrates' chairman, Bernard Barker, warned that fines would get "higher and higher" until hooliganism was stamped out. In London, porter Cyril Howard was fined £50 with £7.20 costs at West London Magistrates' Court. Howard, 54, admitted punching a police inspector in the mouth before the First Division Chelsea–Leeds match. At Bolton, in Lancashire, magistrates' chairperson Marie Mitchell warned football hooligans to stay away from the town. She sent an 18-year-old fan to a detention centre for three months for assaulting a police sergeant at a Third Division game with Bournemouth.

1973 – Soccer Rowdies Sleep in Jail

There was sometimes, just sometimes, the odd "funny" tale. In April 1973, 15 rowdy soccer fans, stranded 300 miles from home because terrified coach drivers refused to take them back – got bed and breakfast at a police station. The fans, from Bournemouth, spent the night on mattresses on the parade-room floor at the station in Halifax, Yorkshire, after the game. Three youths, however, were charged with disorderly behaviour when fans rioted after learning that they could not return home by coach. Two other youths were put up for the night by a police officer and his family. Three teenage girls spent the night at a local children's home. The next day, following breakfast – at their various makeshift temporary accommodations – the fans were put on a train home.

While the incident wasn't the ugliest ever witnessed, things were to become much worse later in 1973. A *Mirror* investigation revealed the terrifying toll of stabbings, beatings and kickings.

One of the most violent seasons in soccer's stormy history was that of 1972/3 and, thankfully, it was coming to an end in May. Stabbings, beatings, kickings and destruction had become almost commonplace at the nation's football grounds. The newspaper set out the shocking truth about the season's violence in the First Division – and published facts that it claimed that even the football clubs and police didn't know. The minister for sport, Eldon Griffiths, said that the findings of the investigation were "a black eye for

British football". But the figures of arrests at First Division grounds during the 1972/3 were not intended as an indictment of any club. They were obtained with the co-operation of the 17 police forces throughout England who had fought against the odds to halt the trend of increasing violence on First Division grounds.

During the season, 3,031 fans had been arrested at First Division grounds. The breakdown, club by club, was given in what the newspaper called "The League Table of Shame". In the season's worst incident, four Millwall fans were stabbed at Everton. In another, volunteer ambulance crews were frightened off the pitch at Newcastle. First Division attendance figures fell throughout the season. There were nearly half-a-million missing fans. Everyone blamed everyone else for the violence. Home fans blamed the visitors and the visitors blamed home fans. But which club had the worst fans at this time? Almost every police force with experience of visiting First Division supporters came up with the same name – Manchester United. One police officer said: "The standard of the supporters has gone down with the standard of the team. We always dread their visits. It is a great pity for a club with such a fine reputation." Chelsea, too, were named frequently, but so were Spurs. On the bright side, Liverpool, Everton and Leeds were consistently mentioned as having the best-behaved fans away from home. Sheffield United – whose home attendances that season were heavily down – finished bottom of the "League of Shame" with 276 arrests. The city's Second Division club, Sheffield Wednesday, also had a bad record. There were 248 arrests at its ground. In his annual report for the previous year, John Richman, clerk to

Sheffield magistrates, revealed that 396 adults involved in soccer violence appeared in court – the highest number recorded in the city. In the "League of Shame", London clubs did comparatively well. But Scotland Yard also revealed the number ejected from the five grounds. It made dismal reading. Chelsea had 1,263, while Spurs saw 889 removed. West Ham had 597, Crystal Palace, 381, and Arsenal, 333. Southampton – the smallest ground in the First Division at the time, but once a hotbed of hooliganism, saw 721 ejected from its matches. However, Southampton were beginning to feel that they were getting on top of the problem – with help from local magistrates who handed out stiffer penalties. Coventry and Ipswich were probably the two centres where the police were best equipped to combat hooligans. Both took "mugshot" photographs of troublesome fans, and Ipswich kept a rogues album – which proved much in demand from other forces. In Coventry, magistrates gave one hooligan fan an unprecedented life ban. Minister of Sport Griffiths was shocked by the number of arrests. He said: "We have these figures for the very first time. I am sure that hooliganism has made a contribution to the decline in football attendances. This is why I supported the 'referees' revolution' so strongly. Foul play and bad manners on the field undoubtedly encouraged violence on the terraces. I welcome the efforts being made to contain hooliganism by football clubs and the police and I look forward to a considerable improvement next season. But there is only one sure way to ensure this. The vast and law-abiding majority of our football fans have a duty to help the police and the clubs in bringing to book the hooligans."

Bob Wall, secretary of Arsenal, which had one of the fewest arrests in London, said: "It is deplorable that the total figures should be so high. I am only glad to see that Arsenal came out well. I am sure this is because we try to impress on them that they support a fine club with a fine tradition – and that hooliganism lets down this tradition." British Rail – once the prime target of football vandals – had managed to stem the destruction. But only at a mammoth cost to the taxpayer. Every week, 2,000 trains carried football supporters through Britain – and 1,600 of those were under police surveillance.

The League table showed – for the first time – the number of home fans and visitors arrested at First Division grounds. Not all clubs had finished the season's matches at the time of publication, but it gave a good indication of the trends. The figures for Manchester City's ground at Maine Road also included the arrests made at the FA Cup semi-final between Wolves and Leeds United. Birmingham City's figures included a number of Aston Villa fans because the two grounds were close to each other. It read:

Newcastle United	22
Arsenal	23
Everton	25
Crystal Palace	39
West Ham United	64
Southampton	80
Leicester City	82
Liverpool	104
Chelsea	120

Birmingham City	125
West Bromwich Albion	125
Stoke City	138
Tottenham Hotspur	144
Coventry City	179
Derby County	180
Leeds United	181
Wolves	195
Norwich City	214
Manchester City	227
Ipswich Town	238
Manchester United	250
Sheffield United	276

This all transpired in the same year as a big fight for safer sport. A major campaign to make Britain's sports grounds safer was launched by the Government on 24th July 1973. Home Secretary Robert Carr appealed to soccer clubs to adopt strict, new safety rules before the Football League season started again on 25th August. The Government's proposals were circulated to sports and safety organizations, so that they could give their comments before a code of practice was issued in the autumn. Laws were to be introduced later to back up the code. Clubs were being asked to consider setting up detention cells for soccer rowdies in the safety shake-up. The clampdown followed a report on Glasgow's Ibrox Park disaster in 1971, when 61 people died in a stairway crush.

Then, in August 1973, spy cameras were used to pinpoint soccer rowdies as game after game was marred by waves of violence and wrecking. Terrace hooligans were picked out by policemen watching a special screening of the Reading v Swindon "friendly" derby filmed by their own TV cameras. A senior officer said: "It means that the days when we could grab only a handful of hooligans while the rest escaped scot-free are over. Now, the whole mob is on film, and we have plenty of time to issue their descriptions and spot them next time." Sixteen youths were arrested after fierce scuffles on the terraces at the Reading match. Many wearing "bovver" boots and heavy belt buckles were turned away before the game began. The spy cameras had the full support of the Reading manager, Charlie Hurley, who said: "The ring leaders should be birched and jailed." Ninety-five Oxford United supporters were arrested after a riot on an intercity train. Doors were kicked down, windows smashed and seats ripped as the fans returned home after the game against Hereford. At the height of the riot, a British Rail guard, Tom Allworth, locked up 40 wreckers in the end carriage – and "marooned" them on the track. He uncoupled the carriage, then walked back along the track for a mile, placing detonators to warn other trains. The coach was then shunted into Kingham, near Oxford, and eight youths were arrested by police. "I had no choice," Tom said. "I could not guarantee the security of the Royal Mail any longer – and my other passengers were terrified." A squad of 25 police travelled on the train to Oxford where a further 87 were arrested. A British Rail Western Region spokesman said: "It was one of the worst cases of vandalism we have had in this region. They were going absolutely berserk." Meanwhile, it was revealed that fans might be banned from the terraces after violent clashes at a local derby between Carlisle United and Workington. One casualty, 19-year-old Ian Townsley, was taken to intensive care.

More was to come. On 29th August 1973, a youth was stabbed in a scuffle between jeering soccer rowdies on a railway station. Police with dogs had escorted more than 100 shouting Charlton fans to the station at Hove in Sussex after their team beat Brighton 2-1 in the first round of the League Cup. The youth, a Brighton supporter, was knifed in the shoulder.

1974 – Soccer Rioter Jailed and the "Battle of Brum"

In March 1974, Leonard Conroy really "went to town" at his first visit to a football match for 25 years. He got drunk, landed in the middle of a riot and assaulted two police officers. The 47-year-old was arrested. He then paid the price for his violent outburst when he was jailed for six months by magistrates at Newcastle upon Tyne. The court was told that Conroy dashed onto the pitch at St James' Park during Newcastle's match against Nottingham Forest in the FA Cup tie. He yelled: "Come on, let's stop the fucking game!" Fans poured onto the pitch, halting the match. Conroy battled with police before he was arrested. He punched PC Alfred Sarin in the face, breaking his glasses. He punched and kicked PC Kenneth Dodds. Conroy of Scotswood, Newcastle, admitted assaulting the two policemen, breaching the peace and damaging a constable's glasses. The court was told that he had had too much to drink. He couldn't actually remember what happened when he got onto the field. Bradley Stevens, for Conroy, said: "It was the first time he had been to a football match for 25 years and he asks me to assure the court that he will never go again." Two Newcastle fans, twin brothers Patrick and Michael Skipper, were remanded on £100 bail. They were accused of assaulting Forest half-back, David Serelia, and of a breach of the peace. A Forest fan, Peter Sisson, 20, admitted a breach of the peace before the game and was remanded in custody for sentencing. Meanwhile, in Manchester, a number of football fans were fined following incidents before and after the Manchester United–Glasgow Rangers "friendly" match the same weekend.

Later that same month, magistrate Graham Hands was an eyewitness to the mindless violence of the soccer "louts". He and his wife were on the terraces at Birmingham when fans ran riot during the match with Manchester United. The shocked JP, who had by this time already fined a number of soccer rowdies brought before his court, said: "I am convinced that I have been far too soft." He added: "It looks as if we need some labour camps where offenders would be made to work a good deal harder than in prison and kept at it all the time. I am sure other magistrates will be taking stronger action from now on. Otherwise, we could soon find it necessary to hold courts at the grounds to deal with people on the spot." Before, during and after the match – which Birmingham won 1-0 – 58 fans were arrested. Scores of people were treated for injuries after the worst soccer violence the city had seen. Six people were detained in hospital – one of them the victim of an attack with a dart. A police inspector had his foot broken as he joined his men in the crowd. Hands, 41, gave this verdict on the "Battle of Brum": "the scenes I witnessed were a bloody disgrace in human behaviour. They were violent lunacy. Until now I don't think I've really regarded football rowdies in the same light as thieves or other criminals. But now I'm convinced that they're worst than most. It was a pitched battle in there. These louts were animals. You needed lion-tamers, not policemen, but the police did a valiant job considering they were heavily outnumbered. At times there must have been 3,000 or 4,000 involved in the trouble. A brick whipped just past my face and hit my wife, Mary, on the leg. She was very scared. Bricks, bottles, beer cans and coins were sailing through the air. And I saw this poor chap just a few yards away get hit by a flying dart. He had to pull it out of his face as it streamed with blood.

"The worst moments came when Birmingham got their winning goal with a few minutes to go. The whole place became hell. Hundreds of Manchester United fans just surged down the terraces, punching and kicking hell out of anyone wearing Birmingham colours. People were knocked to the ground and trampled screaming underfoot. Some were being kicked as they lay there. One father near me had to struggle to hold up his young teenage daughter after something hit her in the stomach, doubling her up.

"I'm not accusing the Manchester United fans of causing all the trouble. I saw plenty of evidence of Birmingham supporters starting trouble too. Obviously, as a magistrate you must try every case on its own evidence. But this convinced me that the law must exact much stiffer penalties for soccer hooligans generally."

Soccer hooligans involved in the Battle of Brum paid the penalty in a tough court crackdown on 19th March 1974. Forty-three offenders were fined a total of more than £1,600 at two special courts in Birmingham. In some cases the maximum fine of £100 was imposed. Several rowdies faced jail terms if they failed to pay the fines. The crackdown by magistrates came just 24 hours after Hands had been interviewed by the press. He had then talked to his colleagues about much tougher measures. Those before the courts – both Birmingham City and Manchester United fans – were involved in clashes before, during and after the match, and charges of using threatening words or behaviour were brought under the Public Order Act. Among the other heavy penalties were fines of between £60 and £90. The magistrates also imposed the maximum £20 fine on several youths charged with committing disorderly acts under a Birmingham by-law. One 17-year-old youth was fined £70 – or 90 days in jail – after the court heard that he had kicked a police horse in the leg and pulled its tail as he ran down a road outside the Birmingham City football stadium. At one point, magistrate Joseph Grainger rebuked a group of youths who were sitting snickering at the back of the court while they were waiting for their cases to be heard. Meanwhile, magistrates were likely to press for stronger legal powers following the call by Mr Hands for stiffer penalties. He was backed by Birmingham councillor Leo Byron, who thought that soccer rowdies should be ordered to do "social work" on Saturdays, helping the elderly, disabled and needy.

Two months later it was reported that Spurs were shamed as their fans started a riot. Tottenham fans ran riot in disgraceful scenes as their team were beaten by the Dutch club Feyenoord in the UEFA Cup final in Rotterdam on 29th May 1974. As Feyenoord went in front in the second leg to clinch the Cup, the fighting fans broke up seats and threw them at Dutch supporters. They also tried to start fires in an obvious attempt to stop the game. Manager Bill Nicholson, appealing over the loudspeakers, stormed: "You hooligans are a disgrace to Tottenham. You are a disgrace to England." Tottenham knew they couldn't afford to concede goals and also fully appreciated that they needed to score after the 2-2 first leg at White Hart Lane, with away goals counting double. In that respect, skipper Martin Peters twice went agonizingly close. The moment Tottenham dreaded came three minutes from half-time when Feyenoord burst through to go into the lead. Ressel made the running, and a shot from Rijsbergen sneaked through. It was at that moment that the Tottenham fans behind Feyenoord's goal were engaged in a pitched battle with rival Dutch supporters. It was a disgraceful scene, wrote the newspaper reports, and followed the Spurs chairman's pre-match appeal for the London club's fans to be on their best behaviour. Ressel made it 2-0 after 84 minutes and Sidney Wale's appeal went unheeded.

By the end of the month the Battle of Rotterdam ended, as the last battered British soccer fans were hustled onto ferries home. But a bitter war of words was still being waged. Dutch fans blamed the British for the trouble that erupted and the British fans blamed the Dutch police for the bloodbath that followed. The Dutch police were inclined to shrug the whole thing off in the cold light of day, but the European Football Union decided to await reports from the referee and the official UEFA delegate before passing any judgement. Rival groups of fans behind one goal began hurling bottles and seats at each other. Hand-to-hand fighting broke out and, after some delay, the police waded in swinging batons. Spurs fans were ambushed by groups of Dutch supporters after the match; there were running fights along the city streets and police gave chase to many groups sporting Spurs colours. By the following morning, the battle was over, with the Spurs supporters having retreated to the ferries and their charter planes while nursing their wounds. Fans who had been rounded up by police were driven straight onto the ferries in police vans. Only three British supporters were left behind – in hospital.

As the shameful sounds of battle died away, the Dutch fired a last jeering salvo, when local newspapers claimed that not only did Spurs lose the match, but that their supporters lost the fight on the terraces. Police Commissioner Jan Donkersloot defended his men against charges of unnecessary violence. He said: "I let my men drink their coffee until the worst of the fighting was over. I didn't want to risk their lives in that hell. Of course they used their batons. What else could they do against iron bars, sticks, belts, knives, chair backs and glass?" The batons, according to the Spurs supporters, were wielded with devastating effect, and the British Rail ferry *Avalon*, steaming into Harwich, looked like a hospital ship as medical staff patched up the wounded fans. Crew aboard the ferry vowed not to undertake any more football charters. The Spurs supporters, limping back to London, gave widely differing versions of the clashes – although nearly all complained of excessive violence by Dutch police. Carlo Abela, 37, from North London, said he was disgusted by the "drunken exhibition" of some young fans who "went mad" when the game began. He said: "They were carrying crates of beer. They were just looking for trouble and weren't interested in the game. They were a disgrace to their club and country." Alec Browne, a veteran supporter from Orpington, Kent, said the troublemakers were "a disgrace to English football". At Harwich, 16-year-old Tony Coe from Tottenham pointed to his swollen, bruised left eye and said: "The police did this – and I wasn't even involved in the trouble. I was trying to help an injured mate outside the ground when a copper ran up and hit me around the head with his stick." Schoolboy, Russ Jones, 15, of Tottenham, was nursing a nose broken, he said, by a police baton. Jones stated: "I was trying to get away from the trouble when they started clobbering me with sticks." Errol Rassin, 23, from Strood in Kent, said he was trying to rescue someone in the crowd when he went down under two policemen. He got up – with a broken leg. Some fans admitted joining in the fighting. At Liverpool Street station, 17-year-old Graham Buckle, of Hornsey, got off the boat train and said: "When the Dutch began throwing bottles, we retaliated. We just stuck the boot in, defending ourselves. I got a few kicks at a copper." One of the fans left behind in a Rotterdam hospital was Bill Freeman, a 25-year-old bookie from Walthamstow, who said: "I hadn't been drinking. Me and my mates just got trapped in the middle when the police arrived lashing out at whoever got in the way." A UEFA spokesman said it would take some time for reports of the incident to reach their headquarters in Switzerland. He said that although Feyenoord, as the home side, were technically responsible for maintaining order, Spurs could face disciplinary action if there was evidence of serious misbehaviour by their fans. Damage estimated at £10,000 was caused during the night of fighting. It was announced that Spurs might be charged with a fine up to that amount by UEFA. However, some commentators thought the club would escape a ban from any future European competitions because fans did not get on the pitch, and the game was not interrupted. Feyenoord claimed that the official UEFA observer, Swiss FA President Lucien Schmidlin, had told them they would not be held responsible for the trouble.

Tottenham chairman Sidney Wale planned to send a public letter of apology to the people of the seaport city for the hooliganism by a section of the club's supporters. Wale said: "I'll never forget this. We have to accept the blame. This must never be allowed to happen again." Defender Mike England, said: "We are ashamed of the fans. We are stunned and appalled at what happened. None of the players saw the riot, but we saw the aftermath, and that was enough."

Commentary following the rioting noted that the Feyenoord stadium in the heart of Rotterdam had the scars to show for a night of rioting by Tottenham fans. The stadium's president, Jan van Haas, said: "The losers are not Spurs. The loser is the game of football." A shattered plate-glass window at the front of the stadium led to the wreckage inside what was, at the time, one of Europe's finest grounds. More than 300 seats, a door and a barrier were destroyed during the pitched battle behind one goal just before half-time. The last of 5,000 Tottenham supporters were straggling home at the end of May. Van Haas said: "It's a miracle nobody died." He continued: "We don't blame Tottenham or their team. And, it has to be said that the majority of their supporters behaved very well. To us, the damage in the stadium and the city, caused by a minority of hooligans is immaterial. The lasting damage is to be the reputation of football. We have videotape of the whole incident. If the European Football Union want it for their official inquiry, they are welcome. I want Tottenham to know, however, that three or four hundred drunken fans will not be allowed to spoil the friendship between the clubs. British teams will always be welcome in Rotterdam. That, of course, includes Leeds if they come here in the European Cup next season." Feyenoord had a closed-circuit television watch on potential crowd trouble spots, and a wire fence surrounding the pitch. These precautions ensured that no fans were able to invade the game. As moats and fences became more and more a possibility on English grounds, the English clubs were told they could learn from the Dutch champions. Spurs, to their great credit, were not in any way attempting to evade responsibility for the savage events.

Bill Nicholson pointed out, however: "You cannot label all of our fans who travelled to Holland as hooligans. My own daughter, Jean, came here, dressed up in the club's colours, with eight of her friends. They travelled by boat from Harwich. But, I know one thing, I'll never again allow her to go in a group that way. My wife has already had a go at me."

The 4s Travel Company director, David Dryer, promised: "In future we are not going to sell terrace standing tickets for games abroad. It is now obvious that this is where trouble starts." One of the players, striker Martin Chivers, stated: "To be honest, we hardly noticed the fighting behind the goal. It is a tragedy that a small section of our supporters got involved in this way. They are a disgrace to the club." The only complaint manager Nicholson had about his team's performance was their finishing. "We missed three excellent chances in the first half."

In the first half of 1974, a Belgian judge warned Britain's soccer hooligans that they could expect no pity in future. Judge Marcel Laurens issued his warning after remanding five Manchester United fans in custody for up to a month, until they stood trial in Bruges. The fans were arrested when British supporters rioted at nearby Ostend, where United were playing the local side in a friendly game. Laurens told reporters, after presiding over the hearing in his chambers at Bruges: "I like watching football, but this hooliganism can't go on. We will show no pity. We intend to make an example so that other British football fans coming to Belgium will realize that they have to behave." He added: "During the summer, we get a lot of trouble from the English. Never the Germans. Never the French. I suppose it's the cheap whisky they can buy on the boat." The five accused fans were driven from court in a red police van to Bruges' 100-year-old prison. There was nobody to help them during the 30-minute hearing. They refused legal aid, and the British consul in Ostend, Robert Clinton-Thomas, did not attend. The five faced charges of assault and causing damage. If convicted, they were looking at up to three years in jail. The accused included Stephen Murphy, 18, from Manchester, Kenneth Parson, 20, from Salford in Lancashire, Vincent Peet, 18, of Ashton-under-Lyne, John Moran, 18, from London and Robert Mahoney, 18, from Manchester. A sixth Briton, Peter Brunt, 23, who was injured in the disturbance, was due to face trial with the others. He had been discharged from hospital in Ostend and taken to Bruges jail. A Belgian was later arrested and charged with stabbing Brunt. Back in Britain, Manchester United fan Leon Brown, of Gloucester, was remanded in custody by Dunstable magistrates, charged with assaulting a steward at Dunstable Town football ground. Meanwhile, new "battle plans" to stop soccer hooliganism were to get a pre-season test when Manchester United visited Hull City. Among the measures were no-beer trains running directly to the ground, at least one closed pub on the City ground's doorstep, closed-circuit TV to watch stands and terraces, and a turnstile blacklist of troublemakers.

In August 1974, Tommy Docherty revealed that he had banned his 18-year-old son from going to Manchester United away games because of the club's hooligan supporters. United manager Docherty said: "My son Tommy has asked to go to away matches but I won't let him – that's how serious I consider the situation. He has promised he would steer clear of any trouble, but I don't want to take the risk." Docherty was talking 24 hours after some of the club's supporters had again been on the rampage before, during and after a match at Orient. He added: "If there is anything I can do or say to help stamp out this hooliganism I will. But there appears to be no answer to it. These people are not supporters. I call them followers. We don't want them. We would like to know how to get rid of them." Docherty endorsed the scathing comments about United's bother-boys by director and former manager, Sir Matt Busby. "The present fines are obviously no deterrent to these louts and sterner measurers must be taken," said Sir Matt. He had made a vain loudspeaker appeal to the warring fans at Orient, and added: "They are only a minority but we deplore their behaviour and want to tell them straight, we don't want your money or your support, stay away." A life ban from watching football was the sentence Orient manager George Petchey urged. "I've never experienced that sort of fear before," commented Petchey. "After that I wouldn't go anywhere Manchester United were playing if I was an ordinary terrace fan. The sort of brutes the police were taking from the ground nearly conquered the world thirty years ago. They're like the Hitlerites all over again – totally irresponsible, ruthless and unbalanced." Goalkeeper John Jackson confirmed that his goal had been showered with broken glass during half-time.

1975 – TV Starts to Play its Part

In February 1975 an action replay trapped two brick-throwing soccer rowdies, a court was told. The 16-year-old Manchester United fans protested their innocence – until they were shown a film of themselves in full fling on the terraces. The catch-of-the-day was screened at the police control centre set up for a Second Division promotion match between Aston Villa and Manchester United. Birmingham police had installed closed-circuit cameras to spy on hooligans at the game. And the two fans, from Halifax, were fined £80 each by Birmingham magistrates. Police sergeant Michael Otley said: "The crowd had been warned before the game that closed-circuit cameras were being used. The operator focused on a stone-throwing section of youths in the crowd and directed the special patrol group to the scene." The two Halifax youths said that they didn't believe the police had cameras – until they were shown the film. Nearly 80 fans were fined a total of more than £3,900 after violent clashes during the match at Villa Park. A police spokesman said: "This was the first time we've used closed-circuit cameras to combat soccer hooliganism." But it wasn't enough of a deterrent, or being installed fast enough.

In May 1975, Leeds United fans went on the rampage as their team crashed 2-0 to Bayern Munich in the European Cup final in Paris. The club, it was reported, might be facing a heavy fine. Bayern won the Cup for the second successive year – with second-half goals from Franz Roth and Gerd Müller at the Parc des Princes stadium. The Leeds fans were angered by French referee Michel Kitabdjian's decisions. He denied Leeds a penalty in the first half when Allan Clarke was tripped by Bayern's captain Franz Beckenbauer, who led West Germany's World Cup team to victory in 1974. And he disallowed a Peter Lorimer "goal" in the 65th minute, judging Billy Bremner to be offside.

This prompted the Leeds fans to rip their seats from their hinges and toss them at the troubleshooting ball boys behind the Bayern goal. Everything sparked off when the ball boys manhandled a Leeds fan who tried to invade the pitch, literally tossing him back into the crowd. When the Germans took the lead the seething Leeds fans started to pelt anyone in sight. One steward was carried out on a stretcher after being struck by a missile. Near the end, the French riot police, in steel helmets and carrying shields and batons, moved in to stop a major riot. The full UEFA Committee were at the match and witnessed the scenes. So Leeds faced an investigation. Before the match Leeds fans stormed through a huge supermarket near the stadium, clearing the shelves of beer, wine and whisky. An employee said: "Many of them were so drunk they were staggering around. Some tried to get away without paying." The police were called and 120 arrests were reported.

At the end of May 1975, a British diplomat involved in the Leeds United soccer riot in Paris was sent home to London. The order was given by Britain's ambassador, Sir Edward Tomkins, who, 24 hours earlier, had apologized to the French for the actions of British fans at the European Cup final. A statement from the embassy said:

"It is true that a junior member of our staff was briefly detained by the French police after the match. Charges will not be preferred against him, but the ambassador has decided that the young man concerned should return to London." The diplomat was a member of the embassy football team and was one of the 30 to 40 embassy staff given tickets to the match. A French newspaper had claimed that a member of the embassy staff had thrown his moped through a chemist's shop window in his disappointment at Leeds' defeat.

A month later, it was announced that Leeds were to call an emergency Board meeting to consider their suspension from European football for a minimum of three years, a sentence that came in the wake of the riot. England's shaken soccer giants had four days to lodge an appeal against the shock sentence announced by the European Football Union from Zurich, following the rioting in Paris. With a strong sense of injustice prevailing at Elland Road, it seemed certain that the Leeds Board would fight the decision.

Leeds expected at most a two-year suspension and a substantial fine – in line with the original sentence on Glasgow Rangers for crowd violence in Barcelona. The sentence for Rangers was halved on appeal. Leeds certainly did not expect to see the door to Europe slammed in their faces until the 1978/9 season at the earliest. Even to return during that season, they would have to theoretically qualify for a European place in each of the next three domestic seasons – or the door would stay closed until 1979/80. It could have meant a loss of £500,000 to the club. It was under this daunting cloud that manager Jimmy Armfield flew back from Zurich on 13th June, to begin urgent telephone talks with chairman Manny Cussins and his directors. Armfield said: "What upsets me is that as a club we were helpless to control a situation on a foreign ground. Yet it's the club and the players and the thousands of innocent decent fans who get hurt. I feel we have got to appeal." Meanwhile, Derby were planning the introduction of identity cards for their fans.

Derby, who were to represent England in the European Cup in the following season, were determined to ensure that their fans wouldn't get them into trouble. Secretary Stuart Webb said: "We have a good record in Europe – and intend to see that things stay that way. I believe that clubs must be responsible for the behaviour of supporters. Anyone travelling with us, at home, or in Europe, must hold a Derby County Travellers Card. And, anyone misbehaving will have his card taken away."

It was then reported that it was "all too easy to claim that Leeds United have been harshly, savagely, unjustly punished by banishment for at least three years from European competition because of the hooliganism of so-called fans over whom they had no control". The article in the *Mirror* continued: "It is also tempting to condemn that severe sentence on a club which will be stunned by the financial implications of the action taken against them by the European Football Union, following the rioting by Leeds supporters at the European Cup final in Paris last month.

"It is almost the equivalent of a sentence of death for a crime they didn't commit – because, make no mistake, Leeds will find it awesomely difficult to maintain the standard they have set in recent years without any money coming through their turnstiles from European competition. It is possible they will take many years to survive the blow that fell on them in Zurich yesterday. It is an ominous possibility that they may never recover. But," said the reporter, "I still cannot condemn completely the attitude and reactions of the European Football Union." The writer said: "They had to act in a way which showed a determination to counter the most frightening feature of football today – the fear that makes fathers refuse to let their kids go to games." It was a fear that made shopkeepers board up their windows and pubs close their doors. The very real fear of someone getting hurt, maimed or even killed because someone else doesn't like a referee's decision or a result was ever present in football. "Leeds," the journalist said, "may, with some justice, claim they cannot be responsible for the actions of their supporters. The European Football Union have now made it plain that clubs in future must accept such responsibility." Even more importantly, they made it clear that fans themselves must recognize the fact. The European Football Union had set an example for British football's own ruling authorities to follow. Every First Division club, for instance, had fears about the damage that might be done during the visit in the following season of Manchester United's supporters. If those fans could be told that misbehaviour on their part would result in the immediate relegation of their team to the Fourth Division it was hoped that this might just prevent any trouble. It was also mooted that if a similar warning were issued to every other club, it might even prevent the trouble across the board.

In September 1975, it was announced that Everton would have a prison for unruly soccer fans on their Blue Streak charter train to Norwich. The train – chartered from British Rail to beat the ban on soccer "specials" – was already a sell-out well in advance of the match. Five hundred fans were making the trip at £3.50 a head, and would find that one coach had been reserved as a lock-up. Everton had banned all alcohol from the train. There would be strict checks on fans trying to smuggle drink aboard. The club, who would be responsible for the security of the train, had 14 stewards and two railway policemen aboard – that was one security man for every 30 fans. But the club weren't expecting any trouble. At Norwich, police would escort the fans direct from the railway station to the ground. Coaches would also unload at the station – and Norwich supporters were being asked to avoid the visiting fans' route to Carrow Road. Nottingham Forest, who were to visit Chelsea, were also running a charter train for members of their own travel club. Commercial manager John Carter warned: "If there is as much as a pound's-worth of damage by vandalism, our trains will be off the rails." First Division Burnley cancelled all charter trains for the rest of the season. Asked by British Rail to indemnify them against any damage, Burnley demanded in return a guarantee that their fans would arrive on time in "clean, comfortable accommodation", and BR refused. Commercial manager Jack Butterfield, speaking on behalf of a club that prided itself on its low incidence of hooliganism, said: "This kind of one-way attitude from British Rail is a load of nonsense. We are right behind any moves to cut out vandalism. But, while we are prepared to give certain assurances, some people apparently are not. Since British Rail seem to want it all their own way, we won't be using them in future. That's how strongly we feel about their attitude." British Rail was beginning to close all the loopholes that would have allowed fans to get cheap travel despite the withdrawal of soccer "specials". There were to be no half fares for children aged three to 14 before kick-off on Saturdays, and even other excursions on weekdays were to be cut. Fears were voiced about a series of "local derbies" to be played on 27th September, including Manchester City v Manchester Utd, Spurs v Arsenal and Fulham v Chelsea. A Football Association spokesman said: "It could result in a lot of violence all on one day, but the matches must be played."

Meanwhile, the question was being asked: "What should we do with the young soccer thugs? Birch 'em, ban 'em, stick 'em in the stocks or pat them on their empty heads and say 'there, there, be good boys'?" The *Mirror* postbag in September 1975 was full with bright and not-so-bright ideas after more violence took place following a Chelsea v Liverpool match. One thing was clear – very few people could take much more of the "mindless thuggery". People on all sides were calling for action. One journalist commented at the time: "I refuse to believe that morons who go on the terraces to chant their foolish ditties are true soccer fans. How can you sing when you are involved and excited by the thrills of soccer?

"I award the first prize of £10 this week to a man who wants to know whatever happened to Britain's sporting spirit." The reader, J Bron, had written: "What on earth has happened to the famous British sporting spirit? I say that as an Ajax fan, who has always been deeply interested in British sport, which is closely followed in Holland. The headlines these days do not make pleasant reading. Cricket fields are dug up and daubed with paint and soccer fans invade the pitch when their team is losing ... Boxing, which had its birth in Britain as the Noble Art, now seems to be unknown to most British youths. Or don't they like man-to-man encounters any more? Even the players are not free from blame, because quite famous footballers are guilty of moaning and arguing nosily with referees. And this, in England, where I was taught that the referee's decision was always accepted – right or wrong. It is all so sad. It is as if the real English sportsmen had gone away and left the country. Those English people who still seem to think their sports fans are well-behaved should realize that in many parts of Europe, as soon as the news comes that English fans have arrived, the police are put on full alert, mobile anti-riot columns are organized and people stay at home indoors. What a change from 1945, when the British were looked up to all over Europe."

1976 – Pubs Call Time on the Thugs

Pub landlords were teaming up against rampaging soccer rowdies it was reported in September 1976. Their strategy was to simply keep their bar doors closed. At least 30 pub managers were taking part in the campaign, it was announced. They wouldn't be manning the pumps between 5.30pm and 8.30pm on Saturday 18th September. The landlords all ran pubs in the centre of Birmingham where 50,000 fans were expected to see the First Division local derby between Aston Villa and City. There was violence in pubs after the previous weekend's local derby between City and West Bromwich Albion. The landlords' leader, Horace Stokes, said: "Something has to be done to teach the louts a lesson. We must look after the safety of our families and staff."

The following month, in October, time was called at a First Division soccer club in a tough new bid to beat the "boot boy" fans. Police chiefs had declared war on drink at matches where trouble was expected – and the first victim of the new clampdown was Coventry City. After police opposition, city licensing justices refused permission for alcohol to be sold in the club's 15 bars during the game with Queens Park Rangers. It followed the arrest of 31 fans the Saturday before during Coventry's match against Newcastle. A close watch was to be kept on the fans at other major Midlands clubs too. Any trouble, and police would oppose drinks licences for the clubs involved. West Midlands assistant chief constable,

William Donaldson, said: "It is well known that alcohol plays a part in football hooliganism." He added: "There is no firm policy to object to licences – it will depend on the evidence of a particular situation."

However, while many hoped that the decade's violence would not be repeated from the 1980s onwards, few could have known of the horrors yet to come.

1982 – Tears for the Man of Peace

"I saw a young man's life ebb away on Saturday after he was stabbed in the heart on his way home from a football match," wrote Harry Miller. There had been nothing to identify John Dickinson as a football fan. He was wearing jeans, a T-shirt, trainers and a quilted jacket. He could have been anyone's next-door neighbour. "It just seemed an awful and indecent way to die – on a grubby North London pavement, beside a battered old car with a hotdog stand in the background," wrote Miller. John had left the game with the rest of the 35,000 crowd after Arsenal's 2-0 victory over West Ham. He was engulfed by a mob of youths in the shadow of Arsenal's Highbury stadium, 200 yards from Arsenal underground station. There were at least 50 youths in the gang. "The savages" came at Miller but he stepped clear, and a woman with a small child was whimpering in fright. Seconds later, another ordinary guy lay fatally injured. The mob swept on, turned a corner and headed in the direction of Finsbury Park. The police, in force and on alert along the road by the underground station, were there within seconds. "Blood was already drenching the front of the young man's T-shirt. There was nothing they could do," continued Miller. Earlier crowd trouble had halted the match. A smoke bomb was hurled into Highbury's North Bank. The game was held up for 10 minutes as coughing spectators were led to the other end of the ground. Arsenal manager Terry Neill bitterly attacked the "mindless morons" behind the violence. He asked: "Where are the spectators of the future going to come from if decent people stay away from the game? I don't know where you go from here. The players, like all of us, are sick of it."

Football Association chairman Bert Millichip said: "We need help. We have learned to expect these things, but not murder after a game." He added: "It's not just a football problem. It's a national problem – and we have to convince the Government of the seriousness of the situation." The FA was to study reports by referee John Hunting and the police before deciding what action to take. Millichip said: "It's a matter about which we have been in very close contact with the Minister for Sport. If a remedy is to be found, it is entirely out of the scope of the football authorities. We can only try and control fans inside grounds – but all this has done is to escalate trouble outside." The detective leading the murder hunt said there had been a poor response to an appeal for witnesses. Detective Superintendent Lionel Stapely declared: "We feel there are a lot more people who would be able to assist us. A lot of football fans can't be pleased with this sort of thing. We thought they would help in a serious matter like this." Arsenal captain David O'Leary had this message for the hooligan murderers: "Stay away. We don't want you. You are spoiling it for the vast majority of decent people who come to football."

Meanwhile, the grieving friends of murdered fan John Dickinson wept on 2nd May 1982 as they gathered at his favourite pub. One of them vowed at The Mawby in Vauxhall, south London: "We'll avenge his death. It was a senseless killing. He hated violence.

We'll get the person who did it. But there's nothing we can do to bring John back." Bachelor John, a fervent Arsenal fan, had stopped wearing the team's red and white colours because he feared getting caught up in terrace violence. On the Saturday he died, he became parted from his friends when a rowdy West Ham mob pushed him from Arsenal's stadium towards Finsbury Park underground station. John, 24, caught a Tube train back to the ground to collect his car. But he encountered more rampaging West Ham fans and was stabbed in the heart. John's father, Tom, told how Arsenal's supporters would gather at the family's flat in Wyvil Road, Vauxhall, before driving to matches. Mr Dickinson said: "John lived for Arsenal. Now he's died for them. Why is it that it's always the innocent bystanders who suffer – the ones who aren't violent?" John's mother, Margaret, said: "He just loved football. He followed Arsenal everywhere, including going to matches abroad. He had supported the team since he was nine." John's room at the flat was decked with souvenirs of his travels with the team.

On 19th May 1982, a policeman who ordered a baton charge against rioting soccer hooligans described the experience as his worst in 33 years in the force. Superintendent John Mellor, 53, said: "I ordered the charge because I feared for the safety and even lives of my men. It was the only way that 80 policemen could deal with 3,000 determined rioters. The fans said they would kill us if they could get over the fence and I really believe they mean it. Some of my men were very upset and frightened." Mr Mellor, who was hurt in the clashes, added: "These were not just kids taking part in the riot. These were men in their thirties who had their children with them." The superintendent was speaking after scenes at the end of the First Division relegation battle between West Bromwich Albion and Leeds United. Thousands of angry Leeds fans battered down a 9ft-high steel barrier to reach the WBA pitch as their team were about to lose 2-0. Six policemen were knocked to the ground in a barrage of missiles. As the fans surged towards them, 80 policemen guarding the pitch were ordered to draw their batons and charge. They were pelted with bricks, bottles and cans as they drove a wedge into the rioting crowd. Police quickly broke up the fighting fans and forced them out of the ground. But they then went on the rampage in nearby streets. Labour MP Peter Shape, shadow spokesman on Home Affairs and MP for West Bromwich, demanded tough action from the Football League.

He said: "It really is about time they put their house in order as far as football hooliganism is concerned." He also urged a ban on the sale of terrace tickets to away fans the following season as the first step in a clampdown on violence. "That will prevent some of the scenes we saw last night," he said. "But we must work towards the idea of all-seater stadiums and doubling the price of tickets in match days." Football Association chairman, Bert Millichip, who was also chairman of Albion, commented: "We are still trying to find the answer to this problem. We cannot allow this situation to continue. There has got to be a very serious new look by the FA and we hope to get some positive direction and assistance from Parliament."

Leeds United secretary, Keith Archer, said: "We deplore what happened. A minority of supporters got out of hand. It is all the more disappointing in view of the fantastic support we have had this season. The next move is in the hands of the FA." But supporters' club chairman, Harry Long, who was at the match, described the riot as "predictable". And, he said, he found it hard to believe that parents with children were involved.

Mr Long continued: "The number of police there was not enough. Had the game been played at Elland Road, there would have been three times as many officers on duty. I think the baton charge was completely unnecessary." He added that the supporters' club would expel any member found to be responsible in any way. Twenty-three Leeds supporters appeared before magistrates following the clashes. They all denied breach of the peace offences and the cases were adjourned until 30th June. Another 22 arrested during the game were released on bail until 24th May. Thirteen fans were hurt when the crowd barrier was pulled down.

In an unprecedented move, it was suggested that football clubs with violent fans should be "put out of business," said Police Federation chairman, Jim Jardine, who continued: "We know the games that are going to have conflict in them. We know the teams who have violent supporters. One way of stopping this would be to put such a price on the employment of police officers that it could make these clubs go out of business."

Jardine claimed that many clubs were getting police at the matches "on the cheap", and felt that if police chiefs withdrew their services, the clubs could not afford their own stewards. He wanted police chiefs to have the power to ban any events that would be a threat to public order.

1983 – Grinning Soccer Thug is Freed

A soccer hooligan who kicked an Arsenal fan on the day he was stabbed to death, grinned as he was freed by a judge on 5th August 1983. Paul Hull, 18, a West Ham supporter, was ordered to do 115 hours' community service. Hull, of Harrow, North London, admitted assaulting Arsenal fan John Dickinson. He was originally charged with murder, but Southwark Crown Court heard that the stabbing would probably remain a mystery. Hull told the police: "I always wear gloves at matches so I don't get hurt when I hit people."

1984 – While Another is Sent to Jail

On 3rd May 1984, a drunken soccer fan who threw a beer bottle onto Nottingham Forest's pitch was jailed for six months. Unemployed builder, Paul Scarrotti, from Nottingham, hurled the missile during Forest's UEFA Cup semi-final against Anderlecht of Brussels the month before. The game was held up and Forest were later fined over the incident.

However, worse was to come in just a few days' time. On 10th May, Brussels was counting the cost after two days of violence and vandalism inflicted on the city by English football fans. While bar owners and shopkeepers swept up a mountain of broken glass, hospitals dealt with dozens of casualties. The clashes before and after Spurs' match against Anderlecht left one London fan shot dead and two other youths wounded by rifle fire. At least 43 Spurs supporters needed treatment for injuries and 141 were arrested. Thirteen were still locked up two days after the violence started and five were expected to appear in court on 11th May to face charges of setting fire to cars, damaging bars and fighting. The Belgian police also suffered in the street battles. One received a broken nose and another a broken leg after they were attacked in a van by fans they had arrested. The youth who died after a brawl was 18-year-old Brian Flanagan from North London. The other shot fans were 19-year-old William Warley, of Biggleswade, Bedfordshire, who suffered from a hand injury, and Paul Adamson,

25, from Borehamwood, Herts, who suffered a wound to his leg. Warley said: "I was coming out of the football ground and suddenly lost my mates. I walked down a nearby street to find them when I heard a shot and the sound of breaking glass. I felt a pain in my hand and suddenly there was blood spurting everywhere.

"Fortunately, there were Spurs mates around who helped me bandage the wound and I went to the police for help." All three Britons were shot with a type of .22 sporting rifle that could be bought over the counter in Brussels for £50. The rifle was the favourite weapon of Belgian criminals and was widely used in sleazy bars to settle arguments. Despite the mayhem, the Brussels police were satisfied that the tough operation they mounted to combat trouble was largely successful. More than 1,000 riot police were on duty and many of the 8,000 Spurs fans were escorted to and from the game. About 1,500 were put in cells on their arrival in Brussels and sent home when the match was over. An official said: "There has been very little trouble really. We seem to have coped with the English." Shopkeepers and bar owners were not quite so happy. English publican, Tom Baker, who had run a bar in Brussels for seven years, said: "The police advised me to shut my pub yesterday, but I never thought English football could stoop so low. Luckily I kept down the damage by serving drinks in plastic cups." His neighbouring café owner hadn't been so prudent. "Who will pay me for all my broken glasses?" she asked. "I will put in a claim to Tottenham Hotspur." The cost of the police operation was estimated at £640,000. Brussels authorities were expected to ask Britain's problem soccer clubs to pay cash or give a guarantee in advance the next time they were to play in the city.

Meanwhile, the violence by Spurs fans was condemned by Premier Margaret Thatcher as "a disgrace to Britain". She offered a full apology to the Belgians. Thatcher was replying in the Commons to Tory MP John Carlisle, who protested about the fans' "mindless violence". He urged the PM to send a message to Brussels magistrates to show no mercy towards the culprits. "If they feel it necessary to keep them in custody for another football season, that would please the majority of the British public," he said. Sports Minister Neil Macfarlane promised an inquiry into the violence.

1985 – "They're Going to Get You, Mr Leftley"

The "yobbo" who ran onto the pitch at Stamford Bridge and tried to attack Sunderland's Clive Walker was about to be "kicked in the groin", figuratively speaking, by the game he disgraced in March 1985. Newspapers read: "At last someone is about to make football hooligan John Leftley pay dearly for his outrage." The court had failed, the players' union attempts to sue him in a private section had been caught up in legal tangles, and Chelsea could only sue for trespass – hardly punishment for the man who said: "I have spent six years watching that bastard Walker, then he goes and scores two goals against us." However, Leftley, a brickie, who told the court he was an accountant, was about to get what he deserved. The Middlesex County FA spotted his "evil" deed and recognized him as a club secretary within their jurisdiction and also a player in one of their leagues. A charge of bringing the game into disrepute was served on Leftley and it was hoped that the Middlesex disciplinary commission would throw the book at him, banning him for life and ensuring he would never be allowed again to set foot on a football pitch to play the game at senior amateur level.

There were those calling for a loss of liberty where soccer violence was concerned. Soccer gang boss, Les Muranyi, and his mob of "young savages" were put behind bars on 21st May 1985. Sentencing them at the Old Bailey, for a rampage that put 40 people in hospital, Judge Christopher Hillard declared: "Soccer violence must mean loss of liberty ... this was organized planned violence which endangered life." The sentences, ranging from five years to five months, brought stunned reaction in court and angry protest afterwards. Mothers wept in the public gallery as their sons were locked up for their part in the violence that tore Cambridge apart in February 1984. The attacks by Cambridge United supporters on visiting Chelsea fans left streets looking like a battlefield. In court, said the judge, the gang presented a sober picture. But, he told the 25 hooligans: "As a mob with drink in you, you presented a different picture." The judge added: "The public is sick and tired of this sort of behaviour. And the public looks to the courts for protection." Muranyi, 25, from Cambridge, admitted the riot and was jailed for five years. Steven Robson, 24, was jailed for four years for wounding a Chelsea fan with a broken bottle. Twenty-three others were sentenced to prison or youth custody for affray. Some of their supporters in the public gallery swore and gave clenched-fist salutes as the sentences were passed. But there were tears from parents. One mother, 41-year-old Mary Togher, was helped sobbing from court after seeing her 19-year-old son get 12 months. She said: "I thought it would be a heavy fine." Chelsea boss, Ken Bates, said later: "Five years should be the minimum", while Cambridge United chairman David Rufton said all 25 louts would be banned for life from the club's Abbey stadium. Les Muranyi, who masterminded the vicious riot, was known as "The General". The window cleaner was determined to wreck revenge on Chelsea fans who routed his army of thugs in 1983. But the battle that followed was only the latest operation by the gang he led for nearly 10 years. He called Friday night meetings with lieutenants to ensure that visiting fans always got an ugly welcome. Even when he was eventually imprisoned, he tried to plot an operation by letter. Described as "meek" in his everyday life, he faced a lifetime ban from his home club.

The year, 1985, had, however, much worse to come. It was to prove one of the ugliest in football hooliganism history. There were deaths on the terraces, but the riot went on. Thirty-nine soccer fans were killed on 29th May 1985 at the European Cup final between Liverpool and Juventus. Most were trampled to death after fences at the Brussels stadium collapsed under the weight of rioting fans. Italians and Belgians were among the dead. Some were believed to be women and children, stated the early reports. Another 600 people were injured, 150 of them seriously. Brussels police at the time said: "We fear the death toll could reach 60 ..." One spectator who survived the carnage said: "I saw a little boy of six or seven whose father was lying dead next to him." Fierce fighting erupted in the Heysel stadium an hour before the match was due to start. The *Mirror* wrote: "Mobs of Liverpool supporters brandishing flag poles and sticks and lighting fires broke down a flimsy wire fence separating them from Juventus fans. A wall and metal crash barriers collapsed as thousands fled in panic on to the pitch.

"At the height of the frenzy, 6,000 people crowded on the field. Rival thugs continued to fight pitched battles on the pitch as baton-wielding police charged them on horseback." A police spokesman described the scenes as sickening and said inside the stadium it was "total war". He continued: "The terraces are littered with

The Daily Mirror

THE MORNING JOURNAL WITH THE SECOND LARGEST NET SALE

No. 1,768.   MONDAY, APRIL 19, 1909.   One Halfpenny.

FOOTBALL RIOT AT GLASGOW: ANGRY CROWD MAKES BONFIRES OF THE BARRICADES AND PAY BOXES.

The Celtic and Rangers players wait on the field at the end of the Scottish Cup final at Hampden Park in April 1909. With the score at 1-1, the crowd was clamouring for extra-time to be played but the officials decided there would be no further play and a large number of the 60,000 present vented their frustrations by starting a riot once the players left the pitch. It was believed to be the most costly riot the game had seen to date, with damage running to around £1,000 after hooligans had set fire to broken barricades.

1960s St John's Ambulance staff help clear bottles from the pitch during the European Cup Winners' Cup semi-final meeting between Liverpool and Celtic in April 1966.

Coach and railway operators began to introduce measures to prevent hooliganism and vandalism as fans travelled to matches. Here, Wolverhampton Wanderers fans on their way to a game at Manchester United in October 1967 are escorted onto their coach by a guard dog.

A hooligan is helped off the pitch by policemen during the 1-1 draw between Fulham and Liverpool in December 1967.

1970s Manchester United fans watch their first match from behind bars on 25th August 1974. The cage was installed to combat hooliganism and prevent pitch invasions, and the home fans celebrated a 4-0 victory over Millwall.

Firefighters attend to a burnt-out railway carriage, which was destroyed by football hooligans after the Luton v Chelsea match in January 1975.

A day of shame for Cardiff, Wales and football as the Wales v Yugoslavia tie in May 1976 explodes into violence, with cans, bottles and paper rolls pouring onto the pitch – closely followed by outraged fans incensed by some of the decisions made by the East German referee Rudi Gloeckner. Welsh midfielder Brian Flynn tries to calm the situation, watched by John Mahoney and (far right) John Toshack.

A friendly match between Glasgow Rangers and Aston Villa was stopped after 53 minutes when drunken fans invaded the pitch in October 1976. A total of 35 people were taken to hospital while around 100 hooligans were arrested.

Scotland (right) fans invade the Wembley pitch following their side's 2-1 victory in the Home Internationals of June 1977. The goalposts were destroyed and the pitch ripped up as thousands of hooligans went on the rampage in celebration of Scotland's Championship triumph. The tournament was eventually ended after the 1983/4 season, with falling attendances, rising hooliganism and the Troubles in Northern Ireland being cited.

Manchester United supporters return to Dover after clashing with French fans and riot police in Saint-Étienne in September 1977. The European Cup Winners' Cup match ended 1-1 but the English fans were heavily defeated by their French counterparts.

A full-scale riot broke out at The Den during an FA Cup
quarter-final match between Millwall and Ipswich in March
1978. Fighting began on the terraces, spilled out onto the
pitch and then into the narrow streets around the ground.

Trouble broke out on the streets of Newcastle when
Sunderland fans arrived in the city in February 1979.
Mounted police attempt to restore order while a police dog
gets stuck into one of the hooligans.

Football hooligans being searched after clashes between rival Arsenal and Manchester United supporters at London's Euston station in August 1979.

This bus carrying supporters to Elland Road was set on fire by rival fans in September 1979.

1980s As football hooliganism intensified in the early 1980s and more diverse methods of identifying those involved were utilized, many of the perpetrators began hiding their faces in an attempt to remain anonymous and evade prosecution.

Trouble flares on the terraces during England's European Championship meeting with Belgium in June 1980. However, the group-stage match at Turin's Stadio delle Alpi was able to be played to completion, with both sides securing a point after a 1-1 draw.

Unfortunately, the violence often spread from the terraces onto the pitch in the 1980s. Here, Luton Town players are attacked following their 1-0 victory over Manchester City at Maine Road in May 1983, which saw the home side relegated to the Second Division while ensuring the Hatters' top-flight survival.

Those intent on violence and disruption at football matches were not bothered about who their actions affected. This young boy is clinging to the fence trying to escape the smoke that is billowing across from the terraces during Everton's match with Stoke City in August 1983.

The Stamford Bridge ground, holding some of the most notorious supporters in the country, became a battlefield on and off the pitch during the second leg of the Milk Cup semi-final between Chelsea and Sunderland in March 1985. The frightening exhibition of uninhibited violence blackened the night – which belonged to Sunderland with a 3-2 victory – the name of Chelsea and the sport itself.

The 1985 Kenilworth Road riot occurred at Luton Town's ground before, during and after an FA Cup sixth-round match between Luton Town and Millwall on 13th March 1985. It was one of the worst incidents of football hooliganism during the 1980s and led to a ban on away supporters by Luton Town, which lasted for four seasons. The ban led to Luton's expulsion from the Football League Cup during the 1986/7 season. The club also began to enforce a membership card scheme, which Margaret Thatcher's Government attempted to have adopted at grounds across England.

Ken Bates, chairman of Chelsea Football Club, is pictured standing behind an electric fence at Stamford Bridge in April 1985. Initially believed to be a successful anti-hooligan device when it was conceived, fencing at grounds all around the country was removed in the aftermath of the Hillsborough tragedy.

Heysel stadium in Brussels, after Liverpool and Juventus fans clashed prior to the 1985 European Cup final. When Liverpool supporters breached a fence that allowed them to access a "neutral" area of the stadium, Juventus fans retreated against a wall, which collapsed. A total of 39 Juventus fans died in the tragedy and hundreds were injured. Officials, trying to prevent further violence, decided that it would be best if the game went ahead, with the Italians winning 1-0.

MIRROR SPORT

DO YOU KNOW THESE MEN?

WANTED

THE HUNT IS ON FOR BRUSSELS RIOT FANS

THESE are 15 faces from the horrifying Brussels soccer riot that left 38 dead and blackened the name of England forever.

CAN YOU NAME THEM?

Liverpool police issued the photographs yesterday after piecing together a "video nasty" from 50 sickening hours of riot film.

They want YOUR help to trap the men involved in the fighting at the Heysel Stadium before the Liverpool-Juventus European Cup Final.

If you know any of the faces, phone the police on these hotlines: 051-708 8772 or 051-777 4944.

The video shows thugs in Liverpool colours hurling missiles, burning the Italian flag and kicking a helpless spectator on the ground.

Other hooligans are seen wielding banner poles like staves or javelins.

A policeman reels back to avoid a missile. Another truncheon drawn, grapples with a fan who hangs grimly on to his scarf.

One scene clearly picks out a thick-set bearded man wearing a T-shirt with the words Emperors of Rome.

Then Detective Superintendent Bill Bergeant, who heads the inquiry, read from a carefully prepared statement. He said: "We have noted a number of men we wish to interview, but have so far been unable to identify.

"I am appealing to these men to contact me."

Mr Bergeant said that 50 people had already been identified from film.

Seven had been taken in for questioning and freed on police bail.

Anyone who had information should contact the police urgently, he said.

One of the youths identified and questioned is 18-year-old Kevin Hughes from Wigan, near Manchester.

He has been seen by millions on TV apparently hitting an Italian fan with a flagpole, at the Heysel Stadium.

But on TV Eye last night, he denied the flagpole attack.

He said: "It doesn't hit him. It's plastic, not metal or anything like that."

Another fan, David Giles from Stoke-on-Trent, was repeatedly seen on the fringes of the violence.

He told the programme: "People came surging through. If I had stayed where I was I would have been pushed over. I had to move along with them."

● Sixteen fans have been arrested after police watched a video of the riot at the Birmingham City-Leeds match in which one youth died.

IF YOU KNOW ANY OF THEM, TELEPHONE: 051-708 8772 or 051-777 4944

The *Daily Mirror* steps up its campaign to find the louts responsible for the riot in Brussels.

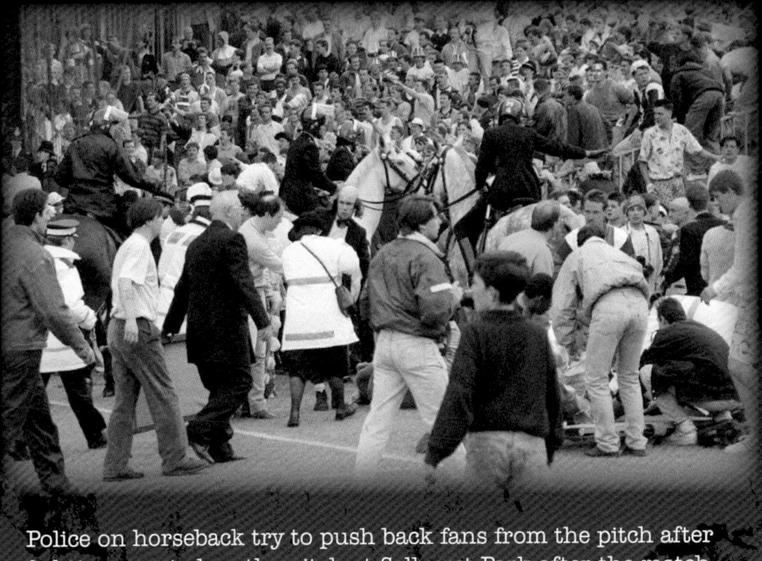

Police on horseback try to push back fans from the pitch after fighting erupted on the pitch at Selhurst Park after the match between Birmingham City and Crystal Palace in May 1989.

1990s Leeds United fans clash with riot police in Bournemouth in May 1990 on what should have been a joyous occasion. The visitors had secured the victory that clinched their promotion to the First Division, but the weekend was remembered more for the violence and destruction that caused over £1million-worth of damage than for the onfield activities.

England fans clash with riot police before their team's game against Holland during the World Cup in Italy, in June 1990.

The press coverage of the events of 15th February 1995 that shamed a nation and its national sport. The Republic of Ireland hosted England in a friendly match but neo-Nazi group Combat 18 – who had split from the British National Party because the leaders felt that political outfit was too soft – were well organized and intent on causing destruction. Jeering and vocal abuse during the national anthems set the tone for the evening, and when an England

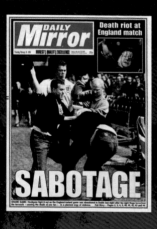

goal was disallowed some English fans began throwing debris – including parts of broken benches – onto the spectators in the lower tiers of the stands. The referee withdrew the players from the pitch but the hooliganism intensified and the game was called off.

England football fans cause havoc in Marseille, France, before the game with Tunisia at the 1998 World Cup.

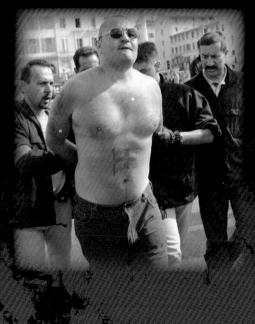

James Shayler was arrested for his part in the fracas. There seemed to be some doubt between various police forces afterwards as to whether he was a known football hooligan but his antics in Marseille resulted in the Leeds United fan being banned from Elland Road for life.

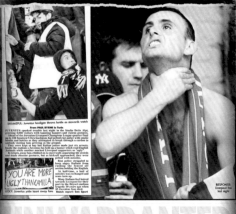

LIVERPOOL'S FEAR AND FURY

SHAMEFUL: Juventus hooligan throws bottle as stewards watch

JUVENTUS sparked trouble last night in the Stadio Delle Alpi, greeting 3,000 visitors with taunting banners and violent gestures.
Ahead of the Juventus-Liverpool Champions League quarter-final up to 100 fanatical Ultra hooligans had pelted riot police with smoke bombs and bottles as they attempted to break through into a zone to ambush visiting fans arriving in the ground.
They were kept at bay but Italian police made just six arrests. Inside the ground some Liverpool fans had to be protected behind barriers while another marked Liverpool supporters on 'sight'.
In return, away fans climbed on to steel walls separating the stands and made obscene gestures, but as kick-off approached, they were pelted with missiles.
Riot police struggled to keep angry Italians from rushing the fenced off section holding the English.
At half-time, a hail of missiles was exchanged and tensions turn up.
Many Italians feel hatred towards Liverpool for their part in the Heysel stadium tragedy 20 years ago when 39 Juventus fans died.
Match report: See Sport

YOU ARE MORE UGLY THAN CAMILLA

UGLY: Juventus yobs taunt away fans

RESPONSE: Liverpool fan last night

UNWARRANTED

150,000 owners of MG Rovers are left without warranties

21st century Despite the fact that the Heysel stadium disaster had taken place 20 years earlier, tensions were still running high between Juventus and Liverpool fans in April 2005. The first match of the two-legged Champions League tie had passed reasonably uneventfully but the return at the Stadio delle Alpi proved to be more of a volatile affair, with Italian fans taunting and goading their English counterparts.

England and German fans clashed in Schlossplatz in Stuttgart city centre after the German v Sweden game at the World Cup finals in June 2006.

Police move into the stands at Ninian Park as Birmingham fans become rowdy during a match against Cardiff City in August 2006. At a subsequent court hearing, Judge Stephen Hopkins described the scenes of violence and disorder at the game as some of the most disgraceful ever seen at a sports ground in south Wales. Cardiff steward Roger Llewellyn-Mortimer was permanently blinded in his left eye when an object thrown from the stands hit him in the face.

The Roma v Manchester United game in Rome was marred by violence in and out of the stadium. Riot police were in place to deal with the fighting fans during the UEFA quarter-final first-leg match in April 2007.

A riot broke out in Manchester's Piccadilly Gardens when a giant screen – that had been set up to show the 2008 UEFA Cup final between Zenit St Petersburg and Glasgow Rangers – broke down before the game.

Tributes are laid on the Ninian Park gates at Cardiff City stadium in memory of Mike Dye, from Canton, who died at Wembley stadium ahead of the England v Wales European Championships qualifier. The England fan who killed Dye was jailed for three years. Ian Mytton, 41, of Redditch, Worcestershire, wept as the sentence – which also banned him from football for six years – was handed down at the Old Bailey. He had pleaded guilty to manslaughter. The court was told 44-year-old Mr Dye died from head injuries after what was described as a single sickening punch ahead of the match in September 2011.

bodies of fans still wearing their team's colours." Another terrified policeman said: "It was like Hiroshima." The newspaper reported: "The thugs carried on stoning each other as emergency services struggled to lift injured fans to safety. And on the terraces Liverpool supporters grabbed Italian flags and banners and set fire to them. After a 30-minute battle, police and dogs forced the Liverpool fans back into their enclosure." Meanwhile, bodies were piled up in a car park outside the stadium and covered with tarpaulins. Two helicopters evacuated the injured from outside the stadium. But rescue attempts were hampered outside the gates by a group of "drunken Liverpool fans without tickets". They fought to get into the ground and attacked ambulances trying to take away the injured. Inside, Liverpool manager Joe Fagan went to the stands wearing a club shirt to appeal for calm. The Juventus players also came onto the pitch and the stadium broadcast appeals in English, Italian, French and Dutch for fans to return to their seats. However, supporters continued to pelt each other and police with bottles, firecrackers, smoke bombs and tin cans. Police were still trying to control rioters when the fencing collapsed. Fifteen rows of spectators fell into a huge tangled heap. A witness told Belgian television: "Most of the victims were trampled under foot. It was terrible. People lay dying on the stands before our eyes." Liverpool fan Paul Souter said the rival spectators should have been more strictly segregated. "It was too easy for the Liverpool fans to get at the Juventus supporters," he said. "I can only think there were too many tickets on sale outside." There were no police separating the two blocks. The match started 90 minutes late after 700 extra police and 1,000 state troopers had been called in; Juventus won 1-0. It is extraordinary to believe that the match was played at all given that so many were already dead and others lay dying where they fell. An emergency number was set up for relatives to call.

Brussels was dubbed "the killing fields of soccer", and the newspapers reported: "Hooliganism doesn't begin to describe what happened ... There was a massacre." The *Mirror* stated: "After years of punishment which never fitted the crimes of English soccer thugs abroad, Brussels was the ultimate shame. We gave football to the world. Now the so-called Liverpool fans give it our national disgrace. No excuses can wipe away the blood which was spilled ..."

Reporters said that whatever the consequences, Britain would have to accept them. Journalists said British clubs should be banned from European football and, if it happened, Britain should welcome the ban, not complain about it. "The Football Association and the Football League [have] consistently failed to grasp the enormity of the threat to the national game," stated one extremely upset reporter. "As they cannot do it, someone else must. It is time to establish a National Football Board to take over the responsibility of safety and crowd control which the FA and the League are incapable of handling," he continued. He further stated: "The deaths last night make up the most appalling event in British football history."

A few miles away from what happened in Brussels, was the battlefield of Waterloo. It was suggested that the riotous events might well have been the "Waterloo" of British football. The captains of the two teams had pleaded in vain with the rioting fans. Liverpool skipper Phil Neal went onto the pitch, escorted by police, and shouted: "Stop this and the match can go on." Italian fans reacted by hurling flaming Molotov cocktails at Liverpool supporters. Neal, who was close to tears, was forced to retreat to the dressing room. The Juventus captain, Gaetano Scirca, also pleaded for calm, but he too was ignored. The soccer world reacted to the slaughter with horror and shame. Former Liverpool captain, Emlyn Hughes, wept as he told BBC radio listeners: "Liverpool's greatest hour has been marred by these animals, pigs, hooligans." Shocked commentator Graeme Souness said: "I think we've seen the last European game by an English team, at least for a very long time." The former coach of the French team Michel Hidalgo said: "This is the defeat of soccer, the end of the European Cup." Doug Insole, FA Council member, said: "I'm sure we are not going to play any part in world soccer soon. No one will want to know us." England manager Bobby Robson, with the team in Mexico, said: "The game has gone sick." England player Ray Wilkins added: "It is a blow to everybody involved in football. It's barbaric. It has nothing to do with football or with the two teams. I never ever expected anything like this." Crystal Palace chairman, Ron Noades, continued: "Giving the police guns is now, sadly, the only answer", while Terry Venables, the English manager of Barcelona, said: "I think the authorities will ban all the English clubs after this." Chelsea chairman Ken Bates remarked: "It's very tragic, and it gives me no pleasure to say I've been warning society for two years about the problem."

Meanwhile, the people of Liverpool watched in stunned disbelief as the tragedy unfolded on their TV sets. The city had been in carnival mood after Everton's triumphant season, and Liverpool's reputation in Europe had always been a proud one. In a packed city-centre pub a woman wept and said: "The name of Liverpool has been dragged into the gutters." There were angry accusations that a Chelsea "wrecking squad" was responsible for inflaming passions in Brussels. Liverpool social worker Pat Chadderton told the *Mirror*: "I have been told by a London social worker that a commando squad of Chelsea fans went to the match to wreck it." Two weeks prior to the awful events, Britain had asked Belgian authorities to turn away British fans who threatened trouble at European soccer finals. Sports Minister Neil Macfarlane wrote to his Belgian counterpart asking for the segregation of rival supporters.

The newspapers, once again, then brought up the "shocking record" of British fans. They cited the suspension of Glasgow Rangers from European football 13 years earlier, after supporters rioted in Barcelona, and stated that: "Since then, the hooligans have blackened Britain's name many times." They also brought up the incidents and rioting by Tottenham fans in 1974, Leeds fans' behaviour the following year, the trouble caused by Manchester United fans in 1977, and the hooliganism in 1980 and 1982. Britain's political leaders united the day after the tragedy in condemning the horror. All blamed Liverpool's hooligan followers and Prime Minister Margaret Thatcher said: "I share the universal horror. It has brought shame and disgrace to the country." Labour leader Neil Kinnock was equally appalled and said: "I am angered and horrified at the senseless violence which led to the tragic death toll." His deputy leader, Roy Hattersley, added: "There is no excuse for such barbarism." Leader of the SDP, Dr David Owen, commented: "This is a devastating blow to Britain's standing in Europe. It must now call into question our future participation in continental football." Macfarlane admitted that British football fans would probably be banned from Europe. "We are now faced with an appalling situation, the dimensions of which will cast a black cloud over European football for ever. This must never happen again." Liverpool MP Eddie Loyden, a lifelong Liverpool supporter, said: "We are all stunned and shocked. It's a night of shame." He continued: "Immediate and draconian measures are now needed to stem further violence." MP David Alton stated that he too felt a sense of shame. "Liverpool has walked tall as giants of European football and not least because of the tremendous good nature of the Anfield fans. This drags the reputation of Europe's finest football club through the dirt."

The violence horrified everyone at the ground who saw it – including many Liverpool fans. BBC reporter Wesley Kerr was just six feet away from the wall when it collapsed, trapping many fans. "There was a crash of masonry about six feet from me ... many, many people must have been crushed to death ... bodies were piled up on each other. A slaughter had occurred," said Kerr. Former England player, Bobby Charlton, who watched in horror from the commentators' box, said: "Maybe after this people will take notice and make sure it does not happen again. It is a disgrace the way people behave when they go to a football match. It has been a disastrous night." Liverpool fan Graham Holland said: "I have never been so sickened in my life. Police and other rescuers had to dodge bottles thrown on the pitch as they tried to get to the injured.

People just lay there. Others wandered around the pitch in a daze. There were dozens and dozens of them who looked badly injured. It was chaos." Mr Holland added: "I could not stay to watch these animals any more. I left the ground without bothering to see the match. I shall never go to a foreign match again." Another Liverpool fan, Dave Swales, 23, said: "There were thousands of Liverpool fans here and just one thousand caused all the troubles. Even after we knew people were dead, the thugs carried on fighting. I can't ever see myself going to a soccer match again. We're talking about a bloody sport! And here we are, with people dying all because of a bloody game." A third Liverpool fan, Frank Barnes, a 49-year-old security officer who had travelled to three European Cup finals with Liverpool added: "I just cannot believe it. After 20 years in Europe and all the games in-between, I just can't accept that Liverpool supporters have done this. Everyone is stunned. What is happening to football and what is causing all this? It is sickening."

Even before the match, Brussels was hit by soccer thuggery. Rampaging Liverpool fans stripped a jeweller's shop of gems worth £150,000. A mob heaved a pub table through the shop window, in the centre of Brussels. Then they looted everything in sight. The raid took place as violent clashes erupted in the Belgian capital. A 22-year-old Liverpool fan was left fighting for his life after he was stabbed in the stomach during a brawl with Juventus supporters, and an Italian was arrested. Fifteen Britons were arrested as a series of bottle and knife fights broke out on the way to the stadium. And drunken louts smashed up the Golden Trawler, one of the best-known pubs in the city. They forced police to retreat under a barrage of more than a thousand beer and Coca Cola bottles. As more police were diverted to tackle the mob, the gem looters struck. Mike Cross, 22, from Alsager, Cheshire, said: "I saw dozens of pairs of hands scooping up everything in sight. They just melted away with dozens of rings, necklaces and brooches ..." But most of the earlier fighting was between rival British fans from London and Liverpool.

On 31st May 1985 it was reported that soccer boss Bert Millichip was ready to ban all English teams from playing abroad. The Football Association chairman, along with FA secretary Ted Croker, jetted home from England's tour of Mexico after being summoned for crisis talks with Margaret Thatcher. Millichip was said to be determined to end the trail of soccer hooliganism which led to the carnage in Brussels. He said: "It could be that we decide not to take part in European football at any level." Thatcher, meanwhile, was looking for a two-year voluntary ban, but Millichip was ready to step in first, with an FA announcement, soon after returning home. He said: "The scale of this tragedy in Belgium is so depressing it is beyond belief. I feel entirely helpless and completely frustrated as to what action can be taken, if indeed the game of football can survive at all." And, he added: "Enough is enough and we cannot put up with these problems any longer." Millichip had the power to make sure the full FA Council agreed to his recommendations with the support of Ted Croker. After seeing televised scenes of the horror from the Heysel stadium he said: "Ted Croker and I have talked unceasingly. We have seriously discussed whether we should take action before anyone takes it against us." The Belgians, meanwhile, were calling for reprisals on English clubs, demanding that Liverpool be thrown out of Europe for the next five years. Belgian FA president, Louis Wouters, explained: "I have asked the UEFA president to impose this punishment because I think it is necessary." Indeed, UEFA president Jacques George bluntly said: "The time has come for UEFA to suspend English teams from European competitions. I know this may not be fair on the clubs who have had no trouble but all have to suffer for the few." Ferdinand Nothomb, Belgium's minister of the interior said: "We have had enough and will refuse to allow any English team on to Belgian territory. There is no time limit on the ban … but it will be for a very long time." Liverpool, Tottenham, Manchester United, Everton, Norwich and Southampton would all feel the immediate chilling impact of expulsion for the following season. And the FA was reported to be withdrawing England from the European Championship qualifying games due to take place in 1987. Norwich chairman Sir Arthur South claimed a European ban would cost English clubs millions of pounds. He added: "To outlaw us would be very sad and very wrong. That would be giving in to the hooligans. I wonder if the mindless minority care about the damage they are doing to the game?"

By Friday 14th June 1985, the net was closing on the ringleaders of the riot in which, by then, it was known 39 people had died. Two top Belgian investigators spent time at the Home Office the day before, then travelled north to meet the special Liverpool police squad seeking the troublemakers. The possibility of extraditing any hooligans positively identified from videos and TV films was discussed. The Belgians had brought films and statements taken from police and witnesses on the night of shame at Heysel. These witnesses were shown pictures of the charge across the terraces by British hooligans, and Merseyside police had established that several known Liverpool and Everton hooligans were at the forefront. But it had become clear that troublemakers had travelled to the match from all parts of England. The Metropolitan Police had picked out a number of notorious London fans, several of whom were known to be connected to the National Front. Detectives had also been helped by the *Mirror*'s special hotline, which was flooded with calls from people prepared to name names. Under the existing law at the time, extradition was possible only in cases of murder and terrorism, but the Home Office promised the maximum co-operation with the Belgian authorities. The European Parliament in Strasbourg also passed a resolution blaming right-wing extremists for helping to stoke the Brussels violence.

In an attempt to help further, the *Mirror* published pictures of 15 people wanted in connection with the soccer riot and asked: "Can you name them?" Liverpool police issued the photographs on 27th June after piecing together a "video nasty" from 50 sickening hours of riot film. They wanted the public's help to trap the men involved in the fighting and gave special telephone numbers for them to call. The video showed thugs in Liverpool colours hurling missiles, burning the Italian flag and kicking a helpless spectator who was on the ground. Other hooligans were seen wielding banner poles like staves or javelins. A policeman was shown reeling back to avoid another missile. One scene clearly picked out a thickset bearded man wearing a T-shirt with the words "Emperors of Rome".

After the showing, Detective Superintendent Bill Sergeant, who headed the inquiry, read from a carefully prepared statement. He said: "We have noted a number of men we wish to interview, but have so far been unable to identify. I am appealing to these men to contact me."

Sergeant said that 50 people had already been identified from film. Seven had been taken in for questioning and freed on police bail. Anyone who had any information was urged to contact police. One of the youths identified and questioned was 18-year-old Kevin Hughes from Wigan, near Manchester. He had been seen by millions on TV apparently hitting an Italian fan with a flagpole. But, on TV, he denied the flagpole attack and said: "It doesn't hit him. It's plastic, not metal or anything like that." Another fan, David Giles from Stoke-on-Trent, was repeatedly seen on the fringes of the violence. He told the same programme on which Hughes appeared that: "People came surging through. If I had stayed where I was, I would have been pushed over. I had to move along with them."

Meanwhile, in Birmingham in June 1985, 16 fans were arrested after police watched a video of the riot at the Birmingham City–Leeds match in which one youth died.

On 5th July 1985, a weeping Liverpool fan was jailed for a year for his part in the soccer disaster in Brussels. As he was led away in handcuffs by armed police, John Ellis, 19, shouted to the Belgian judge: "I am innocent. I did nothing." The sentence – for theft with violence from a hot dog stand at Heysel stadium – was also attacked by his lawyer. The Belgian lawyer maintained: "He has been made a scapegoat for all the British fans who got away after the disaster.

I shall appeal." Ellis was the first person to appear in court since the disaster. But there was no evidence that he had been violent and he had no money when arrested. The hot dog saleswoman who identified Ellis as one of a group of 20 Britons who stole £11 from her stall, said: "He was there but he didn't do anything." Ellis was arrested about 15 minutes before British hooligans started the fatal riot. He was then held in custody until his court appearance. He told newsmen as he was taken away: "All the Liverpool lads in prison here are having a dreadful time. They let us out of the cells only once a day." Ellis, of Liverpool, was said to have previous convictions for theft and damage in Britain. Swiss authorities were also seeking his extradition in connection with the theft of an £84,000 gold necklace in Locarno in 1984. Another conviction for a Liverpool fan came on 30th December 1985. The mother of the young British soccer fan broke down and wept when he was jailed for more than three years by a Brussels court. James McGill, 21, was found guilty of attacking two fans with an iron bar after the riots. As he was led away, Winnie McGill cried out that he was innocent. And her son told reporters: "I was expecting to go home. I was innocent. I'm not too happy at the moment." McGill was accused of attacking two men and was arrested in scuffles that took place after the riot had finished. One of his victims, an Italian hairdresser, spent seven weeks in a coma and would never work again. McGill denied the attacks. The judge said the sentence of three years and four months was meant to reflect the "climate of violence" created by the Liverpool fans, and the dramatic consequences of McGill's actions. McGill was also fined about £200 and ordered to pay the

Italian about £300 as an advance on damages estimated to total £65,000. His lawyer said that with remission and the time he had already spent in jail he could be free within a year. But he also warned that the prosecutor, who called for an exemplary sentence, might appeal for a five-year term. Football Association chairman Bert Millichip welcomed the sentence. "I hope this is going to be a lesson for others sentencing football hooligans to follow," he said.

On 29th May 1986 there was mourning in the Italian city of Turin. But underneath the grief, anger and frustration were mounting. It was exactly a year since drunken hooligans turned what should have been the soccer showpiece of the European Cup final into a massacre. Thirty-two Italians died that day when they were crushed to death in the mayhem at the stadium. Many of the victims were from Turin and a mass for the dead was held in Turin Cathedral, but while the city paused in silent memory of the victims, the agony for their families and for the wounded continued. For most of the millions set aside in disaster funds had still not been paid out. The EEC Commission began paying out from a £120,000 disaster fund around six weeks after the tragedy, but a £3million fund set up by the Belgians was still locked up, bound tightly in red tape. One problem was that the police file couldn't be closed until a decision about the extradition of between 20 and 30 Liverpool fans to stand trial in Belgium on manslaughter charges had been taken. A huge file from Merseyside Police was handed to Belgian law officers three months after the disaster, but, to the surprise of British law officers, no application was made to extradite the suspects. A team headed by Detective Superintendent Bill Sergeant pulled out the stops to identify the troublemakers. He said: "I would have thought that the Belgians would have been ready to make a decision a year after the events." The Belgians had also come in for criticism by lawyers acting for the victims' families. One, Claudio Pasqualin from Vicenzo, said: "They've done nothing. First I wrote to UEFA and they told me to contact the Belgian Football Federation. They told me to contact the insurance company, who said they could not pay out a penny until the court case had been finalized at the highest level." Another lawyer, Domenico Mommoli, said: "The Italian Government said it would pay £5,000 to each of the families 'in need' but not to all the families. This has created great bitterness." He added: "The Italian Olympic Committee promised £250,000 but is still sitting on the money." The Juventus club, at least, had shown real concern for the survivors. A foundation had distributed £400,000 to all the Italian families involved. Margaret Thatcher personally ordered immediate payments of £5,000 each to the families of the dead. But there was nothing for the wounded – people like hairdresser Carlo Cuchene. Juventus fan Carlo, 35, had his head smashed by an iron bar. He was in a coma for seven weeks – as already stated – and could still not use his right hand one year after the attack. Speaking with painful slowness, he said: "My life has been destroyed. I cannot forget and will never forgive. I was awarded £50,000 in court in Brussels by my attacker from Liverpool. Then I found out he doesn't have the money to pay. All the money I have received has been £800 collected by prisoners inside Rome's Queen of Heaven jail."

In September 1986, 26 soccer fans accused of taking part

in the tragedy started a lengthy court battle to avoid extradition to Belgium. The Liverpool fans all faced charges of involuntary manslaughter and were due to appear before London's Bow Street court. The following day, on 16th September, defence lawyers blasted moves to have them extradited; one said the case was likely to become a "show trial". Another warned that they would not get a fair hearing in Brussels. The lawyers hit out after the fans were remanded on bail at the Bow Street court. Belgium wanted to try them for their involvement in the riot and all 26 were jointly charged with involuntary manslaughter of one of the fans, Mario Ronchi. However, the Belgium Government wanted them tried over all 39 deaths. Solicitor Paul Rooney, representing four of the fans, said: "The 26 are scapegoats being used by the Belgian authorities to cover up for their own inadequacies." But Belgium's justice chief, Jean Gol, stressed: "We have a fair system of justice." In January 1986, three Italians went on trial over the riot, but stayed safe at home. None had to appear in Brussels because Italy had no extradition treaty with Belgium. One of the hooligans, a Juventus fan accused of firing a starting pistol, wrote: "Can't come. Got a stomach ache."

The court proceedings did, indeed, prove lengthy. In March 1987, one of the 26 Liverpool fans gave himself up to police. Graham Reevey, 27, added: "All I want is a fair trial. There's talk we could get off on a technicality, but I'd prefer to be cleared by a court." The following month, on 15th April 1987, arrest warrants for the 26 accused were issued in Italy. If any of them were to set foot on Italian soil, they would be put on trial. It was believed that the charge would be massacre. The move came within days of the British High Court's decision not to extradite the Liverpool fans to stand trial in Belgium because of legal blunders. But Italy was unlikely to seek extradition as Britons could only be extradited to face trial if the charges compared with British law – and Britain had no offence of massacre. Fresh attempts were made to extradite the soccer fans on 23rd April, when it was announced that the Belgians would appeal against the decision not to extradite them. On 29th June 1987, the Belgian Government asked law lords to allow the extradition of the 26 fans. All were ordered to surrender to bail by the High Court the following day. The House of Lords hearing was expected to last four days.

On 13th July 1987, five law lords gave the go-ahead for the Liverpool fans to stand trial on charges that could send them to jail for 10 years for manslaughter. They unanimously overturned the appeal court decision. The fans' last chance then was to make a direct appeal to the then home secretary, Douglas Hurd, but even their legal advisers were not holding out much hope. If Hurd did reject their final appeal, the 26 fans would be held in a tough jail, 14 miles from Brussels, possibly for months before the trial took place. Belgium's justice minister, Jean Gol, said the trial, before a panel of three judges, would be a fair one. He added he was confident Hurd would sign the extradition orders. The appeal court had decided in favour of the fans because of a technicality, but Lord Bridge said the rules had been interpreted too strictly. Rex Makin, who represented some of the fans, said that the Lords' decision had been a political one. In September 1987, after home secretary approval, the Liverpool fans were flown to Brussels to face trial there.

It was announced that 15 top Belgian lawyers – some of them famous – had volunteered to defend the 26 fans. They were even prepared to waive their £500-per-day fees. The Belgians thus dismissed worries that the British fans would not get a fair trial, but two Liverpool MPs, David Alton and Robert Wareing, said that Italian fans involved should also be brought to trial.

The 26 fans were to await trial in "more comfortable than the Hilton" surroundings in the airy, centrally heated cells at Louvain prison, which were more like two-room apartments. There was a 12ft by 8ft day room with a table and chairs, and a bedroom for every two prisoners. The cells were equipped with flush toilets, well-sprung beds and a plug for TV. However, Jean Gol faced a storm on 8th September 1987 when he braded the Heysel 26 as "hooligans" before the trial even started. His blunder came in a TV interview as a Belgian air force plane stood by to fly the Liverpool fans to Brussels. He said there would be no soft treatment in prison "for these hooligans". The slip by the head of Belgian's judicial systems caused an immediate outcry among the 26 defence lawyers. One said: "It's very bad for the Minister to publicly find these people guilty of hooliganism before the case starts." But a spokesman for the Justice Ministry said: "Of course there will be a fair and impartial trial." The minister was speaking in English and wanted to refer to the crimes with which the fans were charged. Meanwhile, Hurd said he saw no reason to postpone the extradition of the accused because of the prison riots in Belgium. He said he had full confidence in Belgian authorities to look after the men. He was speaking to reporters on the Isle of Man in response to fears that there could be more violence when the fans arrived at Louvain prison. The Belgians had earlier assured British Home Office officials that the Liverpool fans would be safe in their hands. But parents of the 26 fans claimed that hysteria caused by the jail violence would deny their sons a fair trial. Jean Hurst, chairman of the parents' action committee, said: "I am disgusted that our Government is allowing people to be extradited from Britain while there is wholesale rioting in Belgium prisons."

On 9th September 1987, the accused walked alone on their journey to justice. Only two relatives turned up to wave goodbye – a distraught Unis McKimm, mother of labourer Paul Wright, and her daughter Susan. As 25 of the 26 originally accused Liverpool supporters left Wormwood Scrubs in London in two blacked-out prison vans, they banged on the steel doors chanting a defiant: "We'll be back." The fans were driven at 70mph in a police motorcade to Brize Norton RAF base near Oxford on the first leg of their long-awaited extradition to face charges over the riot. Three hours later, they flew over Heysel before landing at the military section of Brussels airport – where locals had put together a grim welcome. Peering through heavily guarded wire fences, angry spectators waved copies of a national newspaper with the banner headline: "Welcome in Belgium Red Animals." The fans' baggage, which arrived ahead of them, included a Liverpool FC holdall in distinctive red and white colours. Armed with a bag of goodies, mother-of-five Mrs McKimm, 49, had arrived early at Wormwood

Scrubs to pledge her loyalty to her son. But, within minutes of arriving outside the gates of the jail, dark-haired Unis, crumbled into a wreck. She sobbed uncontrollably as a guard told her that her last visit was off. Unis, a care warden for the elderly, said: "I just wanted to kiss him goodbye." Security at Brussels was the sort reserved for heads of state. The handcuffed fans were escorted by armed police to their home for the rest of the year – the city's Louvain prison. A final bid to halt the extradition was abandoned the day before, after a High Court judge refused to intervene in the case. The *Mirror* praised the decision to extradite 25 of the fans, but said that Gol had, through his "hooligans" comment, not only put the men on trial but the Belgium justice system too.

The only Heysel riot suspect still in Britain was jailed on 10th September for "outrageous violence". Jobless Anthony Hogan, 24, would not, however, escape being extradited. A Home Office spokesman said he would still be sent to Brussels when he finished his four-year sentence. Hogan should have flown out with the other 25 fans, but he was kept behind to appear at Liverpool Crown Court where he admitted assault and wounding charges. The court was told how Hogan, of Netherton, attacked four people in a brawl at Liverpool's Lime Street station. He squeezed a burger bar assistant's cheek and told her: "I'll come back and kill you", threw a street cleaner out of the bar and knocked out a bystander, leaving him with horrific injuries. Finally Hogan hit a policeman during a violent struggle. Meanwhile, just hours after the other 25 accused arrived in the Belgium prison, rioting broke out when convicts lit fires and attacked guards in protest at the reported "hotel-style" living conditions for the English accused. However, on 12th September, the fans were branded "savage brutes" themselves after going berserk in their cells. They "howled like wolves", and headbutted the doors of the cells below the Palace of Justice in Brussels, according to one guard. "They really are brutes, savages, beasts," he told a Belgian newspaper. Another guard said the fans behaved in their cells "as if they were Rambo".

No expense had been spared to give the Britons good food. They were sent sandwiches, with a choice of crab, shrimp or tuna salad. Prison officers also laid on new mattresses for the fans, who showed their appreciation by using foul language. "We were under orders not to use our truncheons and to ignore remarks like 'fucking bastards'," said one of the guards. Defence lawyers were becoming concerned about the way some Belgian journalists were whipping up feeling against the fans, however. They feared that headlines, like the one that greeted the fans when they arrived in Belgium, would poison the atmosphere before the fans stood trial. A tough legal battle then began as the 25 were marched before a judge for a five-hour court hearing. Some defence lawyers were planning to appeal to the European Court of Justice against the supporters' detention, if bail applications were refused. All were reported to be calm again at the prison, where rioting had also ceased. However, leave for thousands of police was cancelled in the fear that more rioting would break out. Belgium's prison rules were also changed so that a coachload of relatives could visit the fans in September 1987.

On 12th February 1988, 18 Liverpool soccer fans were released on bail by a Brussels court. But prosecutors immediately lodged an appeal and the fans faced at least another fortnight behind bars while the appeal was considered. Bail of between £850 and £3,200 was set for the 18 and had to be paid before their release. Four of the fans found themselves on their way home from the Belgian jail later that month. They were freed after a court ruled that each could leave the country on £2,000 bail because the trial – expected to start in September that year – had been delayed for so long. The other 16 fans were unable to take up the offer because their families could not raise the money quickly enough. Five had already been released on remand towards the end of 1987. Mrs Patricia Haynes wept as she described how her son, 21-year-old Gary, would not be coming home. "I haven't got the money and there is no way I will be able to raise it."

In October 1988, defence lawyers threatened a mass boycott of the trial. Most of the Liverpool fans on trial headed for home as the 40 lawyers again demanded the right to cross-examine important witnesses. Lawyer Tim Williams said as he left the Brussels court: "The thing's a shambles. We don't know what's going on and we're just sick to death of it." He said the lawyers had told all 24 defendants they were free to go home but would be called the following week to give evidence. Numerous adjournments were called over several days. However, on 26th October, a Liverpool fan was identified in the Heysel trial as "the man with the bulging eyes" who wielded an iron bar on the night of the disaster. Michael Barnes, 23, from Bristol, was recognized by an Italian fan from a photograph published eight months later, the court heard. In a statement read out in court, the witness said: "He was drunk and urging a group of British fans to attack us." Earlier the trial was almost halted by another walkout by 23 defence lawyers. The judge had refused to give them copies of the 47,000 pages of evidence. On 28th April 1989, 14 of the fans walked free – after being convicted over the death of 39 people in the Heysel riot. The trial ended in farce when they were sentenced to three years in jail ... and then allowed to go home. There was chaos and confusion over whether they would serve any time behind bars. Four of the 10 who turned up in court did a runner during the lunch break in Brussels rather than be arrested again. But their great escape had proved unnecessary. The judge said it was up to the prosecutor to order the guilty to be rearrested. But, with a smile, the prosecutor said he would not be ordering any rearrests. The remaining six fans grabbed their overnight bags and rushed for the door. The other four had stayed at home in Liverpool and sent a message that the police would have to come and get them. All 14 were found guilty of involuntary manslaughter and fined £1,000 in addition to their jail sentences. Ten others were acquitted.

Half the jail term was suspended. Allowing for the time they had already spent in prison, that left those convicted with 10 months to serve. The fans' initial relief at being freed turned to anger at the threat: "We'll sue them for wrongfully convicting us." Paul Wright, a 25-year-old builder said: "I'm certainly going to sue. Why should they be allowed to ruin four years of my life, convict me as a killer and then let me go?" John Davis, who stayed behind in Liverpool, was still defiant and said: "I don't think they can do anything. But

I am here and they will have to get me." Prosecutor Pierre Erauw said later: "They will receive an invitation to come to prison. If they say no we may have to bring them here one way or another." Italian Maria Ronchi, whose young industrialist husband died at Heysel, said, at her home near Venice: "I am disgusted that no one will go to jail. All they got was a slap on the wrist for being naughty boys." Otello Lorentini from Florence hit out: "I lost my young son and now I know he died for nothing. It is a total whitewash."

The Belgian Football Association and the police chief in charge on the night of the riot were also found guilty. The judge said the victims' families could bring civil actions for damages against the FA and the convicted Liverpool fans. Lawyers estimated that this could easily come to more than £5million. The European ban following the Heysel riot cost Liverpool FC more than £2million. On average, the Anfield side was making £500,000 a season out of European matches. Players' bonuses and spin-off perks running into hundreds of thousands of pounds had also gone down the drain.

Exactly 10 years after the tragedy, a new stadium was built on the scene of Europe's worst football disaster. The notorious Heysel stadium was demolished by bulldozers. It was replaced by a £12.5million sports ground, and its name was changed to the King Baudouin stadium.

As the 20th anniversary of the tragedy loomed in 2005, Liverpool and Juventus planned a special commemorative service as they joined together to remember the fans who died at Heysel. The two clubs wanted to head off the prospect of any trouble after they were drawn together in the Champions League quarter-final on

18th March 2005. Many people from both cities, and major figures in the UEFA organization, feared "the nightmare scenario" of an explosive clash between the clubs on the raw occasion of a painful anniversary. Liverpool chief executive, Rick Parry, outlined the bond his club shared with Juventus and the steps they would take to ensure Heysel was remembered with dignity and respect. He said: "I really don't think that there will be any problems. I see it as a game of friendship. It is an opportunity for our fans to pay their respects and move on." That was also the view, according to the newspapers, of Juventus. Juventus director, Romy Gai, insisted the tie was a perfect chance to heal the scars of the past. "Heysel is a terrible part of the history of both clubs and we can't forget it – we are obliged to remember it," he said. "This is more than a simple game, but I mean that in a friendly way. We will have the chance to commemorate what happened 20 years ago and show proper respect." It would be the first time that the two clubs had met since the tragedy in a competitive match. There had been one friendly in Turin when Ian Rush moved to the club. While there were still fears that Italian fans had not forgiven their English counterparts and that the game could generate unrest, Parry was to hold talks with Italian directors to discuss the best way in which to remember the victims of the tragedy, and also planned to speak to fans at Anfield to get their views.

The Champions League quarter-final clash did revive a topic that had long been a taboo. It was something that Liverpool players never talked about. It was still raw, still too painful. The horrors of that grim night in Belgium were something that many would never forget. One player, Mark Lawrenson, stated: "I can push the grotesque memories to the back of my mind but they will always be there, always ready to come back to haunt me." He continued: "Amid a background of tragedy and despair, how could something so piffling as a football match have been allowed to be played? Every single Liverpool player sat in the dressing room before kick-off knowing full well that people were dead or dying outside. The sense of grief was indescribable. We didn't want the game to go ahead. Goodness, who would?" However, everyone was solemnly advised by a police chief that if the match didn't go ahead then the trouble could, in all seriousness, escalate. What a choice. Play the game knowing people who had paid to watch were lying dead, or refuse to play and risk further casualties. Lawrenson said: "I remember running out onto the pitch feeling a fraud. How on earth could you even think about playing football when so many Juventus fans had died? It made no sense. It was surreal. This should have been the greatest night of our lives. In fact it was the worst." The injured and the dead were taken to the same hospital as the Liverpool player, who landed heavily on his shoulder and had to have an operation to pin it back. Mark Lawrenson woke to find an armed guard at the foot of his bed for his protection. There were genuine fears of reprisals. There was a huge sense of shame, embarrassment and guilt over what happened, said Lawrenson, "I did not even ask what the score was. I could not have cared less and to this day, I have never seen a second of footage from the game or the night. Someone tells me we lost 1-0." He continued: "A surgeon came in and said there were reporters looking for me. They were looking for someone to blame for the tragedy. It was an awful time. For Liverpool, for Juventus, and for football.

"It took a long time for any of the players involved to come to terms with what happened that dreadful, dreadful night in a foreign football stadium. Since then there has been a lot of bridge-building between Liverpool and Juventus and the Italians can expect a good reception when they turn up at Anfield. I think Liverpool will receive the same treatment in Turin too. There will be a huge sense of occasion. I know that already memorial services are being talked about.

"That would be fitting – a perfect chance to show respect and to remember those who died in the tragedy. It will be a chance for both clubs, both sets of fans, and both cities to grieve and remember what happened 20 years ago. Liverpool fans in particular will want to show their respect. They have always been big-hearted at Anfield and they will do their utmost to make it a warm, emotional night. It would be hard to imagine a more poignant minute's silence and I am positive the Kop will show the greatest respect to the visiting Juventus fans." He concluded: "It was Heysel of course that saw English clubs banned from Europe, costing that year's League Champions Everton a place in the European Cup."

While no one would ever forget the Heysel tragedy, the emotional first meeting between Liverpool and Juventus on 5th April 2005 was a "celebration of all that was good about football," wrote the *Mirror*. The moving scenes were described as "a symbol of how far the game has progressed since then". The emotionally fuelled occasion meant every effort was made to erase the distant memories of 20 years before. However, a hardcore minority of Juventus fans turned their backs when Ian Rush and Phil Neal presented a banner of friendship. But the one-minute silence was impeccably observed, with Liverpool fans remaining silent and the visitors doing their customary clapping. Mark Lawrenson wrote that it was as if the two old clubs could finally move forwards without ever forgetting the enduring memory of those who lost their lives in such a terrible way. But, on 7th April, it was reported that police warned that dozens of Liverpool soccer fans planning to mix with Juventus fans at the match the following week could be walking into a battleground. Many had bought unofficial tickets in the Juventus end in Turin for the Champions League match, a decision which was described as a "recipe for disaster". Some Juventus fans, it was alleged, were threatening revenge for Heysel. The police were right. Juventus sparked trouble in the Stadio delle Alpi, greeting 3,000 visitors with taunting banners and violent gestures. Ahead of the Champions League quarter-final, up to 100 fanatical Ultra hooligans had pelted riot police with smoke bombs and bottles as they attempted to break through a cordon to ambush visiting fans arriving at the ground. They were kept at bay but Italian police made just six arrests. Inside the stadium, a Juventus fan held up a banner which read "English Animals", while another mocked Liverpool supporters as "ugly". In return, away fans climbed onto the steel walls separating the crowds and made obscene gestures, but, as kick-off approached, they were pelted with missiles. Riot police struggled to keep angry Italians from rushing the fenced-off section holding the English. At half-time, a hail of missiles was exchanged and seats torn up. Many Italians felt hatred towards the Liverpool fans for the tragedy. The pall of death and the deep and unforgiving bitterness of loss spilled from banners that hung like shrouds over the three tiers of the bleak concrete bowl of the stadium. Roars of acclamation echoed around the brooding stadium each time the massed ranks of Juventus fans on the Curva Sud unfurled a new message. All of them mourned the dead fans at Heysel. Many spoke of the 39 angels and others revealed the enduring agonies of those left behind. Yet others directed their raw anger at the thin wedge of Liverpool fans sandwiched between the hordes of Juventus followers at the opposite end. "Murderers", read one sign. The Italian fans had obviously been waiting for the opportunity to vent their resentment and their anger for what happened. As the newspapers pointed out, it was obvious that they would try to unleash all their frustrations when they finally got their chance. But, as the *Mirror* stated: "And at the weeping heart of all this grief and this pain and this unrequited lust for revenge lay a terrible and haunting irony. Because the Italian fans were so busy spewing out their disgust for what happened at Heysel, they could not see they are turning into the monsters our supporters used to be." Reporter Oliver Holt wrote: "Only one night earlier, the Champions League quarter-final between AC Milan and Internazionale had to be abandoned after Milan keeper Dida was struck by a burning flare. Within seconds, a hail of flares had rained down on to the pitch." The previous week, Livorno and Lazio supporters fought running battles in Rome, while, earlier in the season, Paolo di Canio celebrated a goal with a Fascist salute. Racist chanting was so commonplace in

Serie A that the Government's sports minister threatened to close down several grounds in 2005 to try to shock the most powerful clubs into action. As Holt wrote: "It all sounds dreadfully familiar. We can all remember the hooligans who ruled our football grounds too. And we can remember the tragedies they caused. Thankfully, we learned a terrible lesson from Heysel. Not soon enough to stop Hillsborough, tragically, but just in time to drag us back from the brink of total football isolation." He continued: "Now it is football in eastern Europe that is scarred by the behaviour of its supporters. And in Spain. And in Italy. If something is not done, the supporters of an Italian club will cause deaths soon and history will repeat itself." Holt concluded: "These two clubs [Liverpool and Juventus] are joined by suffering but the worst tragedy of all would be if the sins of the past are allowed to be visited on a new generation of football fans."

However, Heysel was not the last episode of football hooliganism for the year 1985. A vicious thug was jailed for life on 8th November amid an astonishing uproar in court. Chelsea fan Kevin Whitton, 25, was convicted of riot and assault on a pub landlord, who had a broken beer glass smashed repeatedly into his face. When he heard the sentence, Whitton tried to leap out of the dock at police and the judge and had to be restrained by four prison officers. Friends and relatives screamed and one shouted at a police officer: "You're dead." Whitton's sobbing mother called: "He's a nice boy. He wouldn't hurt a fly." Handing out the toughest-ever sentence on a soccer savage, Old Bailey judge, Michael Argyle, told Whitton: "It is this type of behaviour which has branded an entire generation of

British people in the eyes of the world as being dangerous, violent and outside the law." A second man, Stephen Bowden, 23, who was among a gang who bit off a soldier's ear, was jailed for eight years. Whitton, from New Addington, south London, was at the head of a mob of Chelsea thugs who rioted when their team lost a vital home match against Manchester United. Just five weeks earlier, he had been paroled from a two-and-a-half-year jail term for "glassing" an innocent man. Judge Argyle said: "This was a disastrous error by the Parole Board." After the riot Whitton joined a gang led by the evil "Fat Man" – who was still being hunted by police – that plunged a jagged glass in pub manager Neil Hansen's face. Mr Hansen lost four pints of blood and needed 100 stitches. Bowden, of Kilburn, North London, was convicted of wounding an assistant manager at the pub and causing an affray. Speaking of the life sentence for Whitton, Millichip, from the FA, said: "This will send shock waves around potential troublemakers. I applaud the judge."

The gang, described as blood-crazed, drunken soccer thugs, laughed as their leader bit off a young soldier's ear. As his sister desperately tried to stop the horrific attack she was told: "You're asking to get raped." The hooligans were fresh from a pub brawl in London's King's Road in which the pub landlord was gashed so violently that blood spouted seven feet in the air. Bowden was among the gang which, covered in blood and chanting "war, war, war", piled onto a bus. Hell-bent on violence, they began punching Irish Guards cadet Charles Redmayne, who was with his 20-year-old sister, Eugenie. Charles, 19, said: "A big fat man was leading the aggression. I didn't fight back because it was pointless. Suddenly, the big man grabbed me and sank his teeth into my left ear. He let me go and I saw a piece of my ear fall from his mouth. He shouted, 'I've bitten his bloody ear off' and they all started laughing." Earlier the gang had bought terror to the Henry J Beans pub. As one group of yobs terrorized innocent drinkers, roof tiler Whitton held the landlord while the fat man repeatedly plunged a jagged beer glass into his face. Hansen told the jury: "A gang of eight of nine came in and told me: 'You fucking Americans, coming here taking English jobs.' I asked one of them what I had done to anger him and he said he'd tell me when he had put a glass upside down on my head.

"We exchanged blows, then I was struck in the face with a broken pint glass. It went right through my cheek and smashed into my teeth." Blood jetted high into the air, but two firemen held the 30-year-old's face together and saved him from bleeding to death. After the attack, he faced years of dental work and plastic surgery. The former American Marine said: "I was wounded in Cambodia. But it was at the hands of the British soccer thugs that I thought for the first time, I'm a gonner." Chelsea police then led the hunt for the fat man. Since the rampage they have studied Chelsea crowds at home and away for him. Bowden and Whitton refused to name him. However, Whitton had his life sentence cut to three years in May 1986 after three appeal court judges ruled his sentence as "unjustified". All other commentators said that the much lighter sentence was "a joke".

1986 – Football is Back ... so are the Hooligans

The authorities thought they had hooliganism under control, but in the summer of 1986 the thugs reared their ugly heads when Glasgow Rangers visited Tottenham in a testimonial for long-serving centre-half, Paul Miller.

A friendly it might have been meant to be, but some supporters did not enter into the spirit of the occasion. Fourteen of them were injured and 50 arrested as fights broke out in a corner at the Park Lane end of the ground. The kick-off had been delayed nine minutes to allow many of the 8,000 Rangers followers to get into the ground. That's when the trouble erupted. Some Rangers fans – and they were still allowed in Europe – tried to break out and get at Spurs supporters 20 yards away and separated by a no-go area. Rangers player-manager, Graeme Souness, appealed to the referee to get the match underway so there would be some football to watch.

But, by then, the damage was done and police had to resort to a baton charge to restore order. Ironically, it was Rangers' first trip to London for 16 years. They had not been invited down because most of their previous visits had been scarred by crowd trouble. Rangers' new boy, Terry Butcher, got first-hand experience of how fanatical their fans could be two-and-a-half hours before the match. As he was being driven to White Hart Lane to meet his new team-mates for lunch, Rangers fans recognized him and besieged the car. "They swarmed all over us and were shoving their hands and arms through the car window and begging me to autograph them," said Butcher. Souness, however, kept Butcher on the sidelines; the wraps were due to come off the £725,000-England World Cup star the following day in a friendly against Bayern Munich at Ibrox. Cammie Fraser gave Rangers the lead in a fiercely fought match that swelled Miller's bank balance by around £80,000. Tottenham, who gave World Cup men Glenn Hoddle, Chris Waddle and Gary Stevens a second-half outing, equalized through Clive Allen.

Rioting louts brought more shame on English football on 8th August 1986. A savage battle on board a North Sea ferry left shocked sports chiefs fearing a new worldwide ban on the nation's warring clubs. Clubs had hopes of an early return to European competition following the ban imposed after the Heysel stadium disaster, but with the start of the new season just a fortnight away, a rampaging mob of thugs put English soccer back in the dock. Supporters from London, Manchester and Liverpool on their way to "friendly" matches on the Continent fought a pitched battle with knives, bottles and fire hoses on a ferry bound from Harwich to the Hook of Holland.

The sports minister, Dick Tracey, said the riot could "set us back years". He branded the hooligans as "idiots", and said: "they had no thought for football at all". Manchester United chairman, Martin Edwards, said in Amsterdam that: "This is an absolute tragedy. We plead with our fans not to travel but we cannot enforce it. We are powerless. If the culprits are found they should be locked away." There were fears that English clubs could be banned from playing friendly matches anywhere in the world. But fans sent packing by police after the ferry was forced to return to Harwich were unrepentant. Some, arriving at London's Liverpool Street station, boasted of having given rivals a good hiding, enjoying a great scrap and settling old scores. FIFA, world soccer's governing body, ominously asked for a special report on the riot. It was taunts about soccer's Munich air disaster which sparked the bloody battle aboard the ferry.

The jibes brought brawling Manchester United fans storming to avenge the insult to the memory of their heroes who died in the 1958 crash. Hundreds of terrified holidaymakers watched in horror as they clashed with rival West Ham and Liverpool supporters. More than 150 louts fought with bottles, glasses, chairs and Stanley knives as they rampaged through the luxury Dutch ferry, the *Koningin Beatrix*. The riot left three of the casualties with stab wounds and 15 brawlers were arrested. The owners of Sealink banned all soccer fans from their Harwich services until they showed they could behave. The hooligans heading for the friendly matches had dodged pre-boarding checks by hiding their team colours and splitting into smaller groups.

Police believed the violence might have been planned by the sinister Inter City Firm of well-heeled thugs. Fighting broke out in the bar soon after the new £40million ship – pride of the Sealink ferry fleet – sailed from Harwich. Manchester United fan Tony Canon, 22, from Altrincham, said: "There were Stanley knives everywhere. The stairways near the main bar were running with blood." John Payne,

21, from south London, said: "I was hit by some idiot swinging a knotted rope round his head." Student Stephen Manning, 24, from Kennington, south London, called the rioters, "animals". "By the end of the fighting there was broken glass and blood everywhere," he said. Holidaymakers locked themselves in cabins as the mob fought on the stairways. Carole Cooney, from Liverpool, on holiday with her mother and daughter, said: "There were hosepipes everywhere and the water was coming down the walls. I'm not proud to be British." At 1am, Captain Joost Nargel decided to turn his ship around. She was met at Harwich by police and sailed again after 60 troublemakers were taken off. Sixteen fans were refused entry when the ferry reached Holland.

FIFA were tempted to reimpose the ban on all British clubs playing friendlies anywhere in the world after the rioting on the ferry. FIFA had originally imposed the ban following the carnage at Heysel. The ban was lifted in December 1985, but, after the ferry riot, it looked as though it would be reimposed. Dick Wragg, chairman of the FA International Committee, feared that it could happen. "I sincerely hope they don't ban us again. But we have to face the fact that it could happen. These hooligans make me sick and I don't know what the world is coming to. We thought we had the problem licked – then it crops up again. We have done everything we can and you can't blame the clubs. It's all down to a few hooligans who go looking for trouble." United manager Ron Atkinson said: "We did not publicize the trip and did not lay on any official travel for supporters. But, it is inevitable that information about the games will leak out." The football hooligans drove another "nail into the coffin", with the rioting on the ferry. They dealt a savage blow to English clubs' hopes of being allowed back into Europe in the following season. And they almost certainly knocked a huge hole in the gates for the opening of the Football League season on 23rd August 1986. Who would risk going to a game while the menace was still there? The fans on board the ferry had been "off the leash" for the first time in 15 months but they couldn't resist the temptation to cause mayhem and to terrorize families going on holiday. The fighting was so fierce the ferry was forced to turn around. Glen Kirton of the FA said: "This is obviously a major setback to our hopes of getting back into Europe." Hans Bangerter, general secretary of UEFA, said: "This is certainly not helping the situation for the English clubs. In fact, it has aggravated it a great deal. It's very disappointing, for we had hoped that after all the effort that has been put in, the problem would have been sorted out. We have called for a full report – and we'll act when we get it." Kirton added: "We view this latest outbreak with disgust and disappointment.

"It would be foolish to think that after Brussels it would all work out alright. Some fans have obviously still not realized the importance of behaving properly at all times. There had been 75 friendlies so far this pre-season and there was not a hint of trouble in any of them. Now this comes to set us all back." He continued: "But I would point out that the people responsible travelled as individuals, not on trips organized by any club." Sealink said they hadn't taken any security measures because they had been assured by the clubs no one would be travelling. It was beyond comprehension for the clubs to stick their heads in the sand and think no one would travel.

As a result of other rioting, English clubs were banned indefinitely from a Dutch tournament. It was in reprisal for the hooligans who rampaged through Amsterdam's red light district in early August 1986. Jack van Zanten, main organizer of the city's 711 tournament, said: "These fans haven't learned anything from the Heysel catastrophe. We were shocked by the scope and size of the riots." Supporters went berserk after Manchester United lost their last match of the tournament against Ajax of Amsterdam 1-0.

The following month, a Swedish soccer thug who spent £8,000 following Leeds United was jailed for 28 days after a terrifying blaze riot. He hurled a rock down a terrace as hooligans set a hot dog stand on fire at a Bradford stadium. Leeds United director, Maxwell Holmes, vowed last night: "It won't cost this young man another penny to come and watch us – we're banning him for life." Unemployed Paul Sodermark, 21, had spent the money over two years following Leeds, magistrates were told. He had £30,000 savings in Sweden – and £300 in his pocket when he was arrested. The court was told that fighting broke out among hundreds of youths at Bradford's Odsal stadium. Sodermark was seen rolling a huge rock towards people below him on the terrace. "Luckily it missed," stated the prosecution, "but if it had hit anyone it would have caused serious injuries." Five other youths were remanded in custody accused of grievous bodily harm and insulting behaviour. And, in Exeter, magistrates sent six youths to prison for soccer violence.

More violence, ending in tragedy, was to follow. On 26th September 1986, it was reported that a young policeman's football-fan father died in his arms after being hit on the head by a stone hurled through the window of a minibus by a rampaging mob of louts. Victim Ian Hamilton, and his off-duty son, Robert, had been to the Rangers–Dundee United match in Glasgow with 10 friends. PO Hamilton, 21, said: "A number of youths and a girl came out of the darkness. A stone came through the window and hit my dad. He collapsed. He was breathing slightly, but I knew it was all over. He died in my arms. The group ran off before there was anything we could do." Police said that stoning rival football coaches was a regular Saturday afternoon pastime in Glasgow. At least two other buses were attacked on the same night that Mr Hamilton died. The 41-year-old from Salisburgh, Lanarkshire, was a Rangers season ticket holder. He died only a mile from the ground of Rangers' arch-rivals, Celtic. His wife, Agnes, 43, said: "At least Ian died without pain. It is terrible to think that you can't go and enjoy a football match without something like this happening." She said her husband and his friends never wore scarves or team symbols. "The group who threw the stone would not even have known it was a football minibus," she added. A train crowded with Brighton football supporters was also stoned near a level crossing at Shoreham, West Sussex, and a 35-year-old man was injured. The attack followed a Wednesday night match against Nottingham Forest, but police said there was no evidence to link it with fans. The injured passenger received hospital treatment. At the same time as Mr Hamilton's tragic death was announced, it was also revealed that Luton's Cup tie with Cardiff would be played, but that no one would see it.

The game would be played behind closed doors, with Luton agreeing to ban their own fans as well as sticking by their principle of allowing no away supporters at Kenilworth Road. The dramatic solution to the bitter row between Luton over the Littlewoods Cup match was to be announced on 26th September if talks went well between the warring factions. A four-option proposal had come from Dick Tracey with the prime minister's blessing. The main options included: play both legs at Cardiff, play the first leg on a neutral ground (Watford), play behind closed doors at Kenilworth Road, allow in season ticket holders and/or card-carrying members only from Cardiff. Tracey had called a high-level summit at Lytham St Anne's, the League's headquarters. Luton chairman, David Evans, had chosen the extreme measure of playing the first leg behind closed doors. Clearly, it was preferable to being kicked out of the Cup, and meant that Evans had not backed down over his insistence that "no away fans" would be allowed into the home ground while he was chairman. Evans had reserved his right to take legal action or appeal to the FA should there prove to be a last-minute snag. Things did not get any better, however, elsewhere in terms of hooliganism.

In October 1986, a gang of soccer thugs murdered a 19-year-old rival fan by knifing him in the chest after ambushing him in the street and chasing him for 150 yards. A detective hunting the vicious killers described them as "a pack of wild animals who hunted down their quarry". The 12-strong gang supported Millwall – a club with one of the worst records in football for crowd violence. West Ham fan Terry Burns, and a friend, a 20-year-old Birmingham City supporter, were attacked as they enjoyed a night out in London's West End. They were thought to have run into the Millwall thugs in St Martin's Tavern near Charing Cross railway station. The gang were thrown out by the landlord who said: "I could tell they were looking for trouble." The thugs then lay in wait for the two companions. Terry's friend, who wasn't named, was stabbed in the throat and arm and was said to be recovering in hospital. Terry ran for his life, but was cornered inside the nearby Embankment underground station and collapsed, dying from several stab wounds to the chest. All but one of the killers were white. All were in their late teens or early twenties. At Terry's home, a relative who answered the door to reporters said: "It's time these sick animals were locked away for good."

In other news, police who asked parents to "shop" their sons following the blaze and riot at the Bradford–Leeds match received 120 calls and made 75 arrests. Also in October, burly soccer thug, Terence Matthews, swaggered off to jail after his lawyer told an astonished court that he belonged to the British breed of war heroes. Friends and relatives cheered when an Old Bailey jury decided that Matthews was not the evil "Fat Man" who maimed a London pub boss. Matthews, a scrap dealer from Wandsworth, London, was acquitted of rioting and grievous bodily harm to Chelsea pub manager, Neil Hansen, but was still jailed for four years for causing an affray. As he strolled to the cells he told the jury: "You ain't wrong, you ain't wrong." His barrister, Keith Evans, urging the judge not to jail him, said: "For 1,000 years or so we have needed tough young fellows like this who are prepared to shed blood at the drop of a hat. We would even have awarded them medals for doing their duty. We still have not made any provision for this violent streak that the British have always had. That is why we have always done so well in wars." Chelsea fan Matthews, 26, had a record of violence and previous soccer hooliganism and weighed almost 20 stone when he was arrested, but slimmed down while awaiting trial. He admitted goading Hansen, but denied being the attacker who rammed the broken beer glass in the manager's face. Some of the jury looked shocked when, after returning the two "not guilty" verdicts, they heard of Matthews' previous convictions. At the time of the Chelsea brawl, he was awaiting trial for "bottling" a man in a Wandsworth pub and later got a suspended jail sentence for the attack. Matthews' counsel told the court: "The hunt for the Fat Man goes on." The *Mirror* said: "The lawyer is an ass." They pointed out that a lawyer's duty was to his client, but said that the lawyer who defended Terence Matthews was a disgrace to his profession. Matthews had a terrible record of violence, and Evans – who knew this – was described as "utterly and disgracefully wrong", for suggesting that "we used to find people like this useful when we had wars". The *Mirror* said: "He slanders decent, law-abiding servicemen who fought – and in many cases died – for their country." The article in *Mirror Comment* continued: "He hands to each football hooligan an excuse. He even encourages them to think they are brave. Thugs don't make good soldiers. They are cowards who betray and desert. Bravery is not brutality any more than lawyers are necessarily learned." The newspaper continued: "Matthews is part of a mob which has emptied the terraces, excluded our teams from Europe and shamed the name of British sport throughout the world ... In his misguided zeal, Evans has done society a great wrong."

In November 1986, soccer thugs were caged by a midnight court to prevent more trouble after a town's worst day of violence. Magistrates called from their homes were urged not to free many fans arrested before, during and after Darlington's Third Division local derby clash with Middlesbrough. Some, who had pleaded guilty, were visibly shocked when they were remanded in custody for up to three weeks. In all, 36 of more than 100 arrested for disorder, assault, possessing offensive weapons and drunkenness were locked up. Fines of between £50 and £200 were imposed for lesser offences.

1987 – Non-drinking, Chess-playing Birdwatcher is Named Thug

Baby-faced Terry Last loved chess and birdwatching – and weekends of bloody soccer savagery. The meek, lemonade-drinking clerk in a solicitor's office ran a vicious gang of lawbreakers. Last, 24, was "field commander" of the Chelsea mob of soccer thugs who waged a six-year campaign of terror against other fans and innocent bystanders. No one was safe from the mob, also known as the Headhunters. They slashed people with razor-sharp Stanley knives, they threw a man through a plate-glass window, ambushed and wrecked a coach carrying rival supporters, beat and kicked police to the ground and left calling cards with messages such as: "You have been nominated and dealt with by the Chelsea Headhunters." The gang was smashed after being infiltrated by undercover police in Operation Own Goal. Last and four other louts awaited sentencing after being convicted at the end of a four-month trial at Inner London Crown Court. Ironically, Last wrote what virtually amounted to a prosecution case. He kept a careful record in his diary of the Headhunters' criminal activities and police discovered that he and two other thugs had links with the far right. They found many photographs of Last giving what appeared to be a Nazi salute. They also seized a snapshot of a Chelsea emblem with "Jews die", scribbled inside it. Police further identified material from the National

Front and British National Party. Last had to postpone his wedding because of the trial. He'd met 19-year-old Fiona Stevens through football. Last, travelling back from a match, stopped at Nottingham where she lived. Fiona couldn't believe that Last was the head of a soccer hooligan gang and said: "They say he hit all these people, but he hates fighting. I have been to football with him eight times and haven't seen him do anything wrong. If I thought he had done any of the things they say he has done, I would leave him. But he didn't do anything wrong. I have heard all the police lies." She continued: "He is really, really sensitive. He burst into tears when I hadn't seen him for two weeks after being arrested." Last had relied on seeing her for five minutes every day. Because they were unable to talk, he wrote daily love letters while in cells under the court. Last, from East London, was found guilty of conspiracy to fight and make affray with three others – Stephen Hickmott, 31, Vincent Drake, 24, and Dale Green, 25, who was found guilty of affray and assaulting a policeman with intent to resist arrest. Green admitted causing bodily harm to another policeman. Four men were cleared of the conspiracy charge and also of affray. All nine had denied the charges, claiming the police were lying and giving false evidence.

Victims of the Chelsea Headhunters will never forget the mob's merciless attacks. One, family man Michael Stretton, continued to have nightmares two-and-a-half years after he was knifed by the gang. He needed 140 stitches in his slashed arm and back and he was off work for seven months. He had been waiting outside a pub for friends at Newcastle upon Tyne when a 50-strong mob of Chelsea fans arrived. "They just waded in, kicking and punching."

He said. "I felt a kick in the mouth and fell through the pub door. The next thing I remember was my arm. There was a great big bash and everything was hanging out of my arm." His tendons and muscles were severed. Other men were wounded too. He said: "I used to get nightmares quite often. I was reliving what happened. I still get them now and again, but I'm over it now."

1988 – Britain's Clean Up Soccer Campaign

Sixty suspected football hooligans were arrested in a dawn raid on 29th March 1988 and a clean-up campaign began. The Wolverhampton coup, code-named Operation Growth, was one more triumph for the new policy of co-operation between the police and the football authorities. The battle against thugs on the terraces seemed as if it was being won, and official League inquiries into violent incidents were down from 41 in 1985 to just eight. However, Europe was caught in the grip of what had become known as the British disease. In Italy, soccer violence was now an almost regular occurrence. More than 80 fans were arrested when trouble flared at a First Division match between Inter Milan and Roma in late March. Sixty were charged with criminal damage and violent behaviour after they wrecked a city bus. Five fans, two policemen and a San Siro stadium security guard were injured in fighting before the game. It was also common by this time for knives and coins to be hurled at players. Police responded by raising protective netting around the pitch. In Holland, bomb-throwing fans from Den Haag and Feyenoord sent the Dutch to the top of the "Thugs Table". In the previous season, one match was abandoned as police fought to contain rioting fans, and the Dutch Cup final was postponed and played behind closed doors. The Dutch, following Britain's lead, then increased police presence at games and installed closed-circuit TV.

In West Germany, Cologne and Schalke fans fired flares into the terraces and stoned the police in a major confrontation the previous autumn, while a train was wrecked by Bayern Munich fans armed with knives, flares and stones. Thuggery continued to escalate and the German police knew they were fighting a losing battle. In Spain, Seville fans attacked what they took to be a rival coach only to discover later that it was a pensioners' day trip and that they had killed one woman on board. Fans, who masked their faces, used iron bars and bottles. Riot police, without the benefit of closed-circuit TV, moved in wielding batons. Their tough tactics appeared to be working – for the time being, Spanish football remained a family day out. However, in Russia hooliganism was growing.

Dynamo Kiev fans attacked a train carrying rival fans and Guria Lanchkhuti had their stadium closed after riots. Police increased their numbers at the next game and the rioting fans calmed down. In Portugal, First Division Guimarães had to call their players out of the showers to escort the referee off the pitch after he was stranded for 15 minutes by a hail of stones. There, referees were often the victims of violence. Clashes between rival fans were rare. In Britain, *Mirror* inquiries supported the official view that English football fans – on trial at home and abroad since 1985 – had responded to pleas from the authorities to save the game. An obviously pleased English Football Association spokesman said: "Violent incidents are on the decrease. A ban on alcohol in grounds and the installation of CCTV systems to monitor crowds at First and Second Division grounds have helped."

In Scotland, too, thuggery was on the decline. David McLaren of the Scottish FA said: "Police can also arrest people after the game at their homes if they believe offences have been committed – as appears to be the case in Wolverhampton. Very few people can argue with facts on a video tape."

However, the moves forward weren't all good. A TV producer made a documentary about football hooliganism – by paying a self-confessed thug to be his "consultant", a jury heard on 5th May 1988. Ian Stoddart hired 29-year-old Cass Pennant, an alleged member of West Ham's notorious gang, the Inter City Firm, to help him film Thames TV's *Hooligan*. Stoddart told London's Snaresbrook Crown Court that he could not have made the film without Pennant. The jury heard that Pennant told presenter Sarah Kennedy on one TV show that he was a "retired hooligan". Pennant, from Hackney, East London, denied plotting with others to stir up violence.

On 18th May 1988, eight cleared football fans walked free from court and then joined in a pub knees-up with joyful members of the jury. It was the second trial of alleged soccer louts to collapse within a week because of police blunders. The cleared, Chelsea Eight, were bought drinks by jurors who kissed and cuddled them. One juror even hailed their leader with a Nazi salute. All eight were alleged to have been members of the Chelsea Headhunters. Judge Dennis Lloyd ordered their release after being told that vital police evidence had been tampered with. Moments after leaving London's Knightsbridge Crown Court, they were the toast of the nearby Tattersalls Tavern. Drink flowed freely as they celebrated with three members of the jury. Jury foreman, John Lawrence, a 25-year-old West Ham fan, said: "They are all great lads, not vicious thugs." Another juror, Lorna Kennedy, 19, said: "They're smashing boys. I knew they were innocent." And

24-year-old Millwall fan, Debbie Tilley, added: "I'm really pleased they got off." The six-week trial, estimated to have cost £500,000, ground to a halt when the prosecution said they were not satisfied with the integrity of three undercover police officers. The court was told that irregularities had been found in police logs. The week before, the £2million trial of 11 West Ham fans was also stopped because of doubts over police evidence. The prosecution had alleged that the Chelsea hooligans psyched themselves up by watching violent videos of the Heysel stadium disaster and Brixton riots as they travelled by coach to matches. The case hinged on evidence from undercover officers who infiltrated the gang in Operation Own Goal 2. One alleged ringleader, 26-year-old Stuart Glass, said: "We were accused on a conspiracy, but I feel that the only conspiracy has been by the police themselves." The cleared fans were planning to sue the police for damages. Shadow Home Secretary Roy Hattersley, a keen football supporter, called for a Government inquiry. Scotland Yard ordered their own inquiry into both cases.

On 27th June 1988, a soccer thug tried to dash for freedom – moments after he was jailed for seven years. But prison officers and policemen grabbed Mark Nicholls, 27, before he could leave the dock. Nicholls, his face twisted and red with rage, was grappled to the floor as he tried to throw punches. His friends and family in the packed public gallery shouted angrily and police officers quickly surrounded them to stop them reaching Nicholls during his escape bid. Three other Millwall soccer thugs, all members of the notorious Bushwackers gang, were stunned as a judge jailed them for a total of 22 years. Norman Kent, 27, cursed the judge and screamed: "Eight years? For what?" The other two, John Causton, 26, and Winston Morris, 25, were sentenced to seven years. As each man was sentenced, their families and friends screamed abuse at the judge. Afterwards, Nicholls' mother collapsed outside court and was taken to hospital by ambulance. The jury at London's Southwark Crown Court was told that the four men, part of a mob of about 50 Millwall thugs, invaded New Cross railway station to ambush a train carrying Arsenal and Charlton supporters. Terrified passengers were forced to flee across live rails as the thugs, armed with ammonia sprays, bottles, knives, wooden staves and lumps of masonry, bombarded the train.

The gang ripped benches from platforms to try to smash their way into the "special" train. The four were convicted of making an affray. Judge Gerald Butler, QC, told them: "This was nothing less than a violent attack upon innocent people." Three other men were acquitted. Earlier at the court, two more soccer showpiece trials collapsed because of doubts over police evidence. Seven Millwall fans walked free after the prosecution offered no evidence against them on charges of conspiracy to carry out a terror campaign. Later, the angry fans threatened to sue police for wrongful arrest. One storekeeper, Benjamin Cowan, said: "The undercover police actually suggested we should organize bigger groups to cause violence."

It appeared that Last was not the only hooligan to keep a diary. A soccer thug who wrote a chilling record of terrace violence in his diary was jailed for three years on 16th November 1988. Police charged Jeremy Bodkin, 22, a member of the Chelsea Headhunters, after reading his accounts of two ambushes of rival fans, Knightsbridge Crown Court was told.

1990 – British Sports Minister "Puts the Boot In"

English football fans clubbed and tear-gassed by Italian riot police had the boot put in ... by Britain's own sports minister, Colin Moynihan. That was the angry reaction on 17th June 1990 to Moynihan's quick praise for the "tough and decisive" police action in Sardinia. The gun-toting Italians were accused of brutally crushing a flare-up before the crunch World Cup match with Holland. A handful of thugs, hell-bent on stirring trouble, did go on the rampage, but responsible English fans say police waded into innocent supporters – and they branded Moynihan a "traitor" for siding with the Italians.

Terrified fans caught in the crush shouted: "No Hillsborough, no Hillsborough." Leaders of the Football Supporters' Association compared the ugly scenes with the savagery associated with South African police. FSA organizer John Tummon declared: "It does something to the human soul when you are hit by a police officer after you have pleaded with him not to." A fan stretchered to hospital, 19-year-old Shaun Mayock, from Southport, Merseyside, said: "Three of the police caught me and wouldn't stop hitting. I tried to crawl under a car but got thumped on the head by a rifle butt. Then they came in with the truncheons." The violence flared after 2,000 English supporters set out to march to the stadium from the railway station in Cagliari. Police halted the march as a confrontation with Dutch fans threatened. A full can of soft drink hurled from the crowd hit an officer on the head – and a hail of bricks, stones and other missiles followed. Dozens were injured on both sides in a series of running battles. Police fired tear gas, and clubbed fans with rifle butts and truncheons. Locals offered shelter in their homes to fleeing supporters. Four hundred fans were herded onto a garage forecourt and "made to sit cross-legged like prisoners of war". Sixty were held in police cells until after the drawn game. Five were arrested – none of them ringleaders of the riot. Police discovered a crude homemade bomb in a cigarette packet under one of the England seats at the match – but it was unfinished and did not go off. Moynihan, who flew in for the match but did not see the violence, said in a statement: "I am grateful to the police for their swift, tough and decisive action." The clash meant that the booze ban on British World Cup fans would stay, but Turin, impressed with the behaviour of the Tartan Army, decided to lift the ban on Scottish fans for the match against Brazil. One drinker who wasn't affected by the clubs in World Cup cities was a Milan lawyer who won special permission to buy booze. He told the magistrate: "I don't like football, but I do like a drink in the evening." Meanwhile, Cagliari's vice girls said that fans were so broke and soccer-mad that they were cutting their prices by 25 per cent.

1992 – New Flare-up as England Face Ban

Riot police went into action against British soccer fans again early on 16th June 1992 – as England faced a second humiliating ban from European football over the violence. Three hundred police were called to a massive beer-tented area at Stockholm to stop fighting between 50 English hooligans and Swedish youths. Earlier, police had warned that rival gangs of Swedish soccer thugs had called a truce – so they could put the boot into England fans together. And UEFA president Lennart Johansson warned that football bosses would have to act if clashes in Malmö were repeated. The battle – the third night England fans went on the rampage – started on open land where beer tents were set up, as fans gathered for the match on 17th with Sweden. A few thugs broke through the police cordon, heading for the city centre to attack an ambulance and to break windows. But the massive police presence soon had the clashes under control. A spokesman said: "We were prepared." Police Superintendent Gunner Skold, said the Swedish soccer gangs saw the English as "role models" and would love a showdown. "There is potential for a lot of trouble," he said. England's prized deal to host the 1996 European Championships would probably be scrapped, said UEFA chief Johansson. English top clubs would be outcasts and British clubs could be sent home in disgrace. He said: "If anything serious happens again it might be better if the English fans went home" – the implication being that the team would have to go too. Johansson had favoured allowing English clubs back into Europe, but was feeling betrayed. "We know the English authorities knew about a lot of these bad fans, so why send them over?" he said. "This cannot go on. The English FA must reconsider. It seemed to have the problem under control, but now it has blown up again."

At the same time, soccer hooligan Neil Goodwin was named in court as a ringleader of the riots in Malmö that could have got England banned again from Euro football. Swedish police arrested Goodwin, 24 – who told them he was a Queens Park Rangers fan – after he was identified on video masterminding violence a few days before. Goodwin, a self-employed pipe fitter from Letchworth, Herts, had a record for violence, it was revealed. He was jailed for nine months in 1989 for a vicious gang attack on two men. This time, he faced a 10-year sentence if convicted in Sweden. Goodwin was said to have given the signal for a riot by jumping from the Big Top "friendship" tent at Malmö. But his stunned family and friends denied that the "quiet, gentle" young dad was behind the riots at the European Championships. Patricia O'Neill, 19, mother of his eight-month-old son said: "There is no way he could be a ringleader. He's not the type." Patricia, who said Goodwin had saved over £1,000 for the trip, added: "Neil is a wonderful father to our son. It is not like him to get into trouble. He has settled down and put his past behind him."

His brother, Philip, 22, said: "He's not the sort to be a ringleader. He is not the yobbo type. Neil was not part of any organization supporting the trip. In fact he doesn't support anyone." However, his father Isaac, 54, said: "He is an idiot. Neil was the peaceful member of the family – a gentle sort and the last one I would expect to get into trouble. I feel terrible. I was shocked. I did not think this was my son. He doesn't go to football that often. He doesn't even support one team. He may be involved but this ringleader thing is a load of rubbish. If someone gives him hassle he will defend himself, but I have never known him start it." Earlier it was revealed that Goodwin had been jailed by St Albans Crown Court after he admitted causing grievous bodily harm. The court heard how he was in a gang of eight to 10 men who savagely beat two brothers after an argument in a pub. One needed emergency surgery. At the time, defence barrister Geoffrey Birch said the assault fell into the "lager lout" category.

Meanwhile, Sports Minister David Mellor condemned the Swedish police for allowing cheap beer to be sold to supporters. He told MPs: "England's fans and beer do not mix well. Some are nasty enough to do it on lemonade." Later, Mellor, who visited Malmö, infuriated Scots MPs by referring to "British supporters". It was felt that a clear line should be drawn between Scotland and other home countries.

1995 – Lansdowne Road: Yobs Make War on Peace

A victim of the England fans' riot in Dublin was fighting for his life in February 1995 after being speared in the head by a stake. The missile – which penetrated his brain – was among a hail of makeshift weapons hurled by the mob in the stands of the Lansdowne Road stadium. National Front thugs were blamed for igniting the violence, which forced the abandonment of the England–Republic of Ireland friendly after 27 minutes. At least 50 people were hurt, and another died from a heart attack.

Late on 15th February 1995, friends of the speared fan – who was 31 and from the Midlands – spoke of their horror. Steve Mitchell said: "Our pal is fighting for life because scumbag English hooligans went berserk. We had absolutely nothing to do with the riot, and our pal was hit with some sort of stake object. What happened tonight was absolutely outrageous. We came to Dublin for a bit of fun to see a friendly match." The victim was first taken to St Vincent's Hospital, then rushed across the city to the Irish National Head Injury Centre at Beaumont Hospital. He had an emergency operation on his injuries, which were described as "life-threatening". The hard-core thugs, a group of about 50 skinheads – were among the English contingent in the upper west stand. They threw missiles down on fans and their children sitting below. One terrified Irish supporter, Michael Cronin, said: "A plank with six-inch nails in it came down and landed beside us. The English fans above us in the top tier started tearing up seats and throwing them down." Millions watched on TV as thousands of fans spilled onto the pitch desperately trying to escape the yobs. The thugs were giving Nazi salutes, screaming anti-IRA slogans and waving Union Jacks daubed with "NF".

A senior officer of Ireland's Garda said: "We have no doubt that this whole terrible episode was pre-planned by the National Front. We had been on the lookout for these boot boys throughout the day. The English authorities had warned us that hard-core troublemakers were on their way over." England manager Terry Venables said: "It was absolutely disgraceful. I don't know how the National Front supporters got the tickets." Ireland's manager Jack Charlton was in tears as he tried to remonstrate with fans. The atmosphere had been bad from the start, with the English fans taunting the Irish: "No surrender to the IRA." The home fans replied: "You'll never beat the Irish." The England mob ripped up wooden seats and hurled them at the police, pelted players with coins and baited officials who steamed across in an attempt to restore order. The referee took the players off the pitch as the missiles rained down. England captain David Platt was the last to leave, and was begging English fans to behave. Police had to stop Irish fans from running across the pitch to take on the English supporters. Among the VIPs at the match who witnessed the riot were Irish President Mary Robinson and opposition leader, Bertie Ahern. Mrs Robinson was sitting in a stand opposite the riot scene – but police took no chances and immediately gave her an armed escort out of the ground.

A task force of 100 Irish police gave England's soccer thugs "a hiding" in the aftermath of the Lansdowne Road riot. They lashed out with batons flailing as they launched a charge against 200 England supporters. Many of the fans fled back into the stands battered and bruised. A senior source within the Irish police forces told the *Mirror*: "About a hundred riot police gave these boys a lesson they will never forget. They taunted us and thought they could take on the law as well as everyone else. Our men were instructed to give them a hiding they wouldn't forget." Later, police in riot gear overcame the yobs again after they were herded by train to the ferry port of Dún Laoghaire. Five hundred hooligans tried to run amok, but cops hustled them onto two ferries. Crossings had been cancelled because of the Force 10 gale, but Irish authorities overruled weathermen and ordered the boats to sail to England in appalling conditions. It had been the peace game that turned to war. The match was to be played out against the background of the political struggle for an end to conflict in Ireland. But the mood was set right from the start as both National Anthems rang out to a hail of abuse from fans. The National Front-led English mob continued with chants of: "No surrender to the IRA." Worse trouble seemed inevitable – and the Irish police had been warned. By mid-morning, 30 hours before kick-off, they were told by undercover detectives in Britain that known soccer hooligans – some of them NF members – were Dublin-bound. The Irish police assured their British counterparts they could handle the situation. In the event, drunken brawls erupted all over Dublin before the match as groups of England fans – supporters of different clubs at home – clashed with each other. Ninety minutes after the game was abandoned (in the 27th minute), many fans were still at Lansdowne Road, and police waded in to give them a taste of their own medicine. The officers did not hold back.

But it was too late. An undercover detective in Manchester spelled out how the warnings were flashed to Dublin before the match. He said: "We warned the Garda what was likely to happen and offered our assistance in identifying troublemakers as they entered the ground, but the Irish police didn't want to know. They said they could handle it themselves." For 24 hours before the match, there had been a massive undercover operation, involving members of Britain's National Intelligence Football Unit, at airports and sea ports around the UK. But the major focus was at Manchester airport, from where most fights take off for Dublin. Police identified 30 known hooligans who caught flights, and passed the information to Dublin. On one occasion they even made rival fans travel on different flights to avoid trouble in the air. The Manchester detective said: "We had specific information which we passed on, including the fact that there was likely to be a pitched battle in Dublin between fans from Leeds and Oldham." It was regarded as a return bout following a fight between them earlier in the year. "We also had good information that Leeds followers would stir trouble with Manchester United fans, taunting them about Eric Cantona. We identified known National Front troublemakers among those travelling to Dublin."

The detective continued: "Our information was that rioting would start almost immediately after the National Anthem had been played – and we weren't too far out. The problem is we weren't there in Dublin either to identify the hooligans and prevent them from getting into the ground. It was frustrating because we couldn't stop these hooligans from going to Dublin. The only way we could have prevented them from leaving was if they were wanted on a warrant or in connection with inquiries."

The National Criminal Intelligence Service said in a statement: "Our Football Intelligence unit has been in regular contact with the Garda in the weeks running up to this game. We have provided every assistance with intelligence and travel information. We were aware that disorder was planned to happen within the football ground. Following the disorder, we will be co-operating with the Garda to offer them every assistance." The majority of England fans went to Dublin by ferry. And 500 of them faced atrocious conditions as they sailed back from Dún Laoghaire. Angry scuffles broke out at the port as some fans were marched to the ferries from trains and buses that had brought them from Lansdowne Road. In one incident, a TV cameraman and his equipment were pushed to the ground. A number of Irish police officers and other security men travelled with the fans to England.

The FA of Ireland planned its own investigation. It was criticized for seating the English contingent in the upper west stand, knowing that if trouble started Irish fans seated below would be threatened. There had been no previous hooligan problems at Lansdowne Road, as Irish fans were renowned for their good behaviour. The mayhem, however, was a grim reminder of the shameful record of England's fans. TV pictures of them hurling missiles from the stand could have prevented England hosting the European Championships the following year. England had been awarded the high-profile event despite the history of violent behaviour by fans. However, England's failure to make it to the finals in America in 1994 at least spared the FA from the prospect of further disgrace.

The *Mirror* said: "Today's soccer yob is the product of a couldn't-care-less society. He lives wild for today because he sees no future tomorrow. He thrives on scenes such as those at [the] Irish friendly because he hates everything foreign. Organizations like the National Front attract him with their cruel prejudice. The yob is living out his own version of the 'Tory dream'. He spends his life in the poor housing estates of forgotten Britain, hearing nothing but the warped ideals of a Government obsessed with greed. Respect for himself or others, is unknown.

"That's why 100 idiots were able to deny millions the right to watch the England–Ireland match. Our police and football authorities are very good at containing trouble inside the ground. But the real problem is very much wider – a group of young men who believe there's only one way to prove how tough they are – by getting drunk and causing trouble." The paper continued: "They live on poor housing estates which daily become more deprived. And they are daily subjected to 'gimme, gimme, gimme' ideals. Most people who do go abroad respect other people's cultures and traditions. But the soccer yob just burns with a passionate hatred of all things foreign."

The newspaper stated that something had to be done before it was too late, and said that a two-pronged attack was what was needed. "We must show that we won't tolerate this behaviour from anyone. And that includes soccer stars like Eric Cantona. We've got to foster the idea that it's patriotic to identify troublemakers to the authorities." The *Mirror* also said: "We must punish offenders severely by depriving them of doing what they like most. So, lock them up, take away their freedom to attend the football matches they pretend to love. But we must remind ourselves why they behave like this. They are nearly all born of poor parents, have little education, even less money and see no future. So they live accordingly."

Alan Ball, a World Cup winner on England's proudest day in 1966, condemned the "mindless yobs" who rioted in Dublin. The Southampton manager said: "These people should be sent away for a considerable spell of time." Ball, a 1966 colleague of Ireland boss Jack Charlton, continued: "You could see the anger in Jack's face." Alan Shearer, England striker, said: "It's a sad night for football, a shame for soccer. The players are very disappointed and there are some who have family up there in the stands watching." Niall Quinn, Irish star, commented: "It was a horrible night. The violence was as bad as I've ever seen. We've got to get rid of the scum." David Platt, England skipper, said: "I am disgusted and appalled, I cannot believe that a game has been stopped by what has happened off the pitch. Five or 10 years ago we were renowned around Europe for the sort of thing that has happened tonight. Now this will get written about once again – not just in Europe but around the world." Alan Ball said: "This was the night that finally put England in the gutter of world football. I have watched more than one hundred internationals, but I have never before witnessed an England match abandoned because of the obscenities of our so-called supporters. England have now forfeited the right to stage next year's European Championship. Even in a season of sleaze, nobody believed that the game could smell any worse. But at Lansdowne Road, England once again became the lepers of world football.

"And I lay the blame firmly at the door of the Football Association. The game has reeled from one crisis to another, from the Bruce Grobbelaar bribe scandal to the Paul Merson cocaine confession, with riots thrown in along the way. But this was the pits. It made you sick to your stomach to be English."

"They are scum," said the Irish supporters suffering the distress of evacuating the stand after a full-scale riot caused the abandonment of Terry Venables' seventh match in charge of England. The FA was accused of failing to send out the right messages in handling the wave of disorder. Eric Cantona had been banned only until the end of the season pending an FA inquiry, but Alan Ball felt he should have been shown the door at Old Trafford immediately for his kung-fu kick on a Crystal Palace fan, regardless of the provocation. Paul Ince had been allowed to carry on playing for England even though he had been arrested and later released on bail, while Dennis Wise withdrew from the England squad because he was found guilty of assaulting a cab driver and damaging his cab. A referee was attacked by a fan and shielded from assault only by quick-thinking Blackburn goalkeeper Bobby Mimms. Thugs scarred an FA Cup tie at Millwall, and then, in the replay at Chelsea, dozens of mounted police were needed to separate warring supporters. Where was the FA? There were no charges, no unreserved condemnation, no convincing leadership, said Ball. The result was that England's first away fixture under Venables was allowed to be accompanied by 1,500 fans. Ball continued: "Hooliganism was once an evil that infested our game for far too long before the Government took any action. Only when Margaret Thatcher watched the news of a riot at Luton was there any real move to curb the violence within the stadiums. Naturally, the FA will fight to preserve their right to stage the European Championship. They lost millions through failing to qualify for the World Cup finals in the United States." It was believed that an Irish goal in the 22nd minute is what sparked the outrageous behaviour. There was also complete shock and indignation that English fans had shown no regard to the threat they posed to women and children in the crowd.

Soccer yob Terence "Tez" Hosking should be birched, his furious father said on 16th February 1995. Retired Ted Hosking said he felt "sick with disgust" when he picked up the *Mirror* and saw his hate-filled son and two pals beating up a fan during England's shame in Dublin. Ted, 63, from Cumbria, said: "I'm deeply ashamed of my lad. He looked like he was giving someone a real hiding. In my book, he should be given a good hiding too. I'd like to see him birched. I've always believed in an eye for an eye and a tooth for a tooth and he's let me down badly. He's always been a soccer fan." Ted said his 30-year-old son had not been in touch since the violence flared, although he had phoned his sister. The lout was also believed to have been present at the Heysel disaster. One of his pals, Graham Posselthwaite, was convicted of involuntary manslaughter. The labourer steered clear of his terraced home in Kendal, but local publicans branded the stocky hooligan as a "head case" and said he was a known troublemaker. One said: "He's all right when he's sober, but he's a madman with a drink inside him – steer clear." A barman told how Hosking was banned from a pub for a year for throwing glasses, and said: "He always ends up blasted." The tearful father of an England fan facing a stabbing charge said: "My boy's no yob." Michael Williams, 23, was remanded in custody in Dublin over the attack on a bar worker before the match. But his father, John Williams, said: "Michael is a gentle giant who's never hurt anyone. He's told me he had nothing to do with the attack – and his friends say the same. He was very upset and in quite a state." Williams was a high-flying sales manager with his father's international electronics firm and was used to jetting around the world on business. In another story, shocked Michael Kearns identified his brother, Stephen, as one of the hooligans attacking a fan in the *Mirror*'s front-page picture of those responsible for the riot in Dublin. Michael said: "I was stunned when I saw the photograph. It has all come as a terrible shock. My parents are terribly upset." University graduate Stephen, 23, who worked as an insurance clerk, was believed to still be in Ireland when his picture was published. He phoned home just after the riot to tell his parents he hadn't been arrested. But he had to face the music when he returned to his parents' home in Harborne, Birmingham. Michael added: "My parents will probably be having a stiff talk with Steve. My mother has been crying with worry since she saw the violence on TV. She still can't believe it." He added: "It is up to Stephen whether he wants to give his side of the story." Michael said his brother had been a Villa fan since he was a youngster and had travelled to Wembley regularly to see England play. Another hooligan caught out was Paul Kieser, who begged a judge to free him from Dublin's Mountjoy jail. Weeping, Kieser was arrested at the height of the riot, held overnight in the jail, and had to fend off killers and junkies out for revenge. "Please don't send me back there," he wailed. He begged tearfully and said that he was a "responsible person" in Ireland on company business and would not try to leave the country if given bail. Moments later, Keiser, from Fareham in Hants, white-faced and shaking was sent back to Mountjoy accused of causing a riot, criminal damage, threatening and abusive language, and breaching the peace. He was joined by Steven Smith from Scunthorpe, Humberside, who was also refused bail. Smith, 27, was charged with criminal damage and carrying an instrument with intent to endanger life. The judge also refused the hooligan's application for legal aid. Paul Dodd was thrown out of the country; he had actually been banned from all UK grounds the year before. Mark Conway was fined £300 for breach of the peace and ordered to leave Ireland. David O'Loughlin and David Hodgeson, both from Rochdale, were fined £75 each for breach of the peace in Dublin's city centre. Paul Bowman from Donnington, Oxford, was arrested for fighting at matches but not charged. Bowman lunged at reporters and was held back by his mum – who told him off for swearing.

Soccer hooligan Shaun Philpot confessed his shame and vowed he would never again go to an England football match. The 24-year-old from West Byfleet, Surrey, who admitted hurling missiles from the top of the stand, said he couldn't explain why he got involved. Several TV viewers spotted Philpot hurling objects from the upper stand. He said: "I just lost my head when it all started and began throwing things along with everyone else. I am so ashamed. Our behaviour was deplorable." He went on: "It was a terrible scene. I have never known anything like it. Everything that happened was shameful and I regret my part in it. I can't deny my involvement, but I can't explain why I did what I did. I just got caught up in the atmosphere with everyone else." Shaun, who didn't work because he suffered from kidney trouble, added: "I have just come out of hospital and I am not a strong person. I am not inclined to violence and I don't know what came over me."

The *Mirror* tracked down the soccer thug seen by millions of telly viewers throwing a plank during the match riot in Dublin. Skinhead Jason Ankers, 23, said: "I admit it. It was me who threw the plank." But Ankers and other soccer thugs could not be arrested by British police because the offences happened in Ireland. The *Mirror* tracked the soccer yobbo down after calls from readers who recognized him on TV video film taken at the match. Ankers lived in southeast London and the newspaper found him working in an off-licence in Balham. Customers watched as the *Mirror* photographed him and confronted him with his violent behaviour.

It was revealed by police that extremists from the neo-Nazi group Combat 18 stirred the Dublin violence. Special Branch officers from London, Manchester and Liverpool learned as far back as the year before that thugs planned a new wave of havoc at football grounds. There was a real fear that maniacs were planning to take guns onto the terraces. They then studied a report that one Combat 18 thug took a gun into the stands during the Spurs v Blackburn clash in February 1995. Undercover officers learned that a series of meetings to plan the violence had taken place in Manchester and east and south of London. A Special Branch source said: "There is an orchestrated plan by a new hard-core group to spread violence at club fixtures and internationals. A network of thugs is travelling around to any game in Britain looking for opportunities to start trouble. We know that the violence in Dublin and the trouble that flared at the Chelsea v Millwall Cup replay are linked. Some of the same faces cropped up at both grounds.

"There are new, worrying aspects to this. Many of these yobs are involved in the drugs underworld and are getting their hands on guns. We hear rumours of planned shooting attacks on rival groups. It is a terrifying scenario." Combat 18 was a splinter group that broke away from the British National Party, which it regarded as being "too soft". Police said that it had infiltrated the terraces at clubs such as Chelsea, Millwall, West Ham, Crystal Palace, Birmingham City, Aston Villa, Cardiff City, Newcastle and Middlesbrough. The Special Branch officer said: "They are using the old National Front trick of recruiting disaffected white yobs via the football terraces and then involving them in their racist attacks."

Football squad officers were on full alert after warnings that Combat 18 activists attached to Millwall planned to start violence at the Cup tie with QPR at Shepherd's Bush. One London football fan who knew hard-core hooligans said: "What happened in Dublin had been talked about for the past two weeks. They are neo-Fascists and connected to Combat 18. They are complete headcases. They were saying there was going to be trouble and that Combat 18 was going to go out there. They were going to do Nazi salutes and the 'no surrender' thing." The fan continued: "They said they were going to rip up the seats as soon as they got in to the ground to use them as missiles. You would have to do some pretty nasty things to get their confidence. They just want to hurt. At the Dublin match they were fighting English supporters as well as Irish. At the Tottenham–Chelsea match one of them had a gun. This Saturday they are targeting QPR and Millwall. They probably won't go into the ground – they're not too worried about watching the games."

Police, by this time, had uncovered a complex underworld of communications between rival gangs. They included "fliers" and handbills by groups such as the Chelsea Headhunters, the Arsenal Gooners and Millwall's notorious F Troop. "Wanted" posters gave details of individual rival fans, including their pictures. Gangs also produced "business cards". West Ham's notorious Inter City Firm used calling cards bearing the slogan: "Congratulations – you have just met the ICF", which they pinned to victims they had just beaten up. After the Dublin riot, calling cards were found around the ground with slogans including "No surrender to the IRA" and "England invasion of Dublin 1995". Another, thought to have been copied from Glasgow Rangers gangs, insulted the pope. Ringleaders, known in the gangs as "generals", who lead the rounds of racist chants and songs, had been identified by police. One football officer with the British Transport Police said: "Before a game they plan the exact times when they will burst into a round of Nazi salutes or charge opposition terraces. The information is passed by word of mouth, but there is a good network. The top yobs communicate across the country by phone. We have just raided London gang leaders and found diaries with the phone numbers of leading rival yobs in other cities, some in Holland and Sweden."

A former gang member said: "The hard-core troublemakers would carefully plan their disruption. They would know exactly where each of them would be in the ground. They'll have a timetable worked out in advance. They are very clever. They know how to exploit the most sensitive times during the match. For instance, they will try and start trouble during the National Anthems. If that doesn't work, then they wait for the first goal. And, that's exactly what happened in Dublin." As the *Mirror Sport* revealed, there was a real problem looming for the European Championships, with a system that virtually guaranteed black-market tickets available for thugs. Even more crucially, why were known violent hooligans allowed into the match? Among those identified by the *Mirror* were "savages" with criminal records for soccer-related violence. The highly effective police Football Intelligence Unit had spotted some in advance, but the Irish police rejected their offer of help. At that point, the FA should have called off the friendly international. It was outrageous, according to the *Mirror*, that it continued to take the risks so lightly. But, then, the *Mirror* wasn't surprised by the inaction of an organization that had consistently failed to deal with its own players and their violence. Vinny Jones brutally assaulted a *Mirror* reporter in front of an FA official. All the FA did was to call for yet another report. However, it was mooted that the FA's inability to get tough was only a contributory factor to what happened in Dublin. The blame lay solely with the "beasts" who ran riot. Unlike earlier reports, the *Mirror* claimed these men were living in comfortable homes, on comfortable incomes and that "their behaviour is due entirely to their own frightening psychopathic mentality". After Dublin, the FA did set up phone lines in order to encourage the capture of the thugs. The *Mirror* said: "Each of them must be tracked down, punished and banned from ever again going to a soccer match. Not just in this country, but throughout the world. That is the only way for football violence to be stamped out. And stamped out it must be if we are not to surrender to soccer terrorism."

A brilliant teenage soccer star who turned his back on the game and joined a gang of thugs was in the crowd at Lansdowne Road. Former England schoolboy international, Gary Breeds, was highly rated 10 years previously. He spent the night of the match chanting in the stands with his hooligan chums. Breeds had been on Sunderland's books in the 1980s and played for England Under 15s, but he was thrown out of the English squad under a cloud. He remained at Sunderland in the youth team and played in the reserve side, but he failed to hit the big time and drifted into a life of thuggery. Breeds was one of the ringleaders of the Seaburn Casuals Firm. He was arrested and banned from every soccer ground in Britain, but that didn't stop him travelling to Ireland. His thuggery began when he was still playing at Sunderland. He was filmed leading a pitch invasion at York City. According to Jim Morrow (England schoolboy coach and the Sunderland Youth Development Officer), he had been "a unique kid". He had had a great future ahead of him but he was involved with a "bad" crowd and his club couldn't control what he got up to.

A little boy's fear of the soccer louts turned to loathing and contempt. TV cameras had caught James Eager's features frozen with bewilderment as violence erupted around him at Lansdowne Road. Eight-year-old James gripped his father's hand and asked what was happening. Once he knew, he had a firm opinion about the thuggery of the yobs more than twice his age. "It was a disgrace," he said. He told ITN reporters: "I felt very frightened." James had been taken to the match by his father Shay, a former goalkeeper for Shamrock Rovers, as a special outing. They ended up running onto the pitch for safety. Meanwhile, it was reported that England fan Andrew Norris, who had been speared in the head, was off the danger list following an operation.

Not long after the events in Dublin, the *Mirror* unmasked a "Face of Shame" and introduced their "Shop a Yob" campaign. The exclusive pictures of hooligans showed yobs happily watching the game before covering their faces with balaclavas when the trouble started. The newspaper set up a special hotline so that readers could phone in if they identified any of the yobs they featured. The next on the hit list were the bungling Irish soccer chiefs who played right into the hands of the thugs, purely for greed.

It was reported that they sold hundreds of tickets returned by the English FA to home fans – knowing they would be sitting among the 4,000-strong English fans. The revelation caused serious embarrassment to the Republic's ruling soccer body. Sports Minister Bernard Allen told the Dublin Parliament that 3,800 tickets were supplied to the English FA. Of those 1,164 were sold in England and 1,200 were returned to the Irish FA and sold. What happened to the other 1,436 tickets was then said to be under investigation by the

Irish Government and the police. Hundreds of Irish fans, including young children, were seated in the middle of English yobs in the upper west stand. However, Sean Connolly, Irish FA chief, claimed that they knew nothing of any secret plans by hard-core thugs.

The FA followed the *Mirror*'s initiative and introduced their "Shop a Thug" campaign in the battle to beat the hooligans. The major "new war" against violence on the terraces came in a direct appeal to ordinary fans. They were being asked to turn in the mindless yobs who transformed Lansdowne Road into a battlefield. The FA even received assurances from FIFA and UEFA that no pressure would be put on England not to host the European Championships.

Meanwhile, two drunken soccer hooligans who shamed England were given jail terms thanks to the *Mirror*, said the newspaper. They were arrested at their bed and breakfast in Dublin after a reader recognized them and tipped off police. A Dublin judge studied the picture of the men, Steve Kearns and Steve Sloan, attacking an Irish steward. Then he sentenced them both to two months in the notorious Mountjoy prison. Later they were freed on £100 bail each, pending an appeal. They both admitted to causing a breach of the peace. The young men then tried to sell their story in return for help to get them home. The *Mirror* declined. They then faced further humiliation when the skipper of the Sealink ferry refused to allow them and 10 other England fans on board. Seven other soccer louts were confronted with a barrage of contempt and cold fury after being nailed by the *Mirror*. Two were given jail sentences, others faced the hatred of neighbours who wanted them kicked out of town, one – a civil servant – was sent home from work as bosses probed his behaviour, and another was banned by his favourite club. The hooligans would have preferred to sneak home, hiding their shame, but five were identified after they were pictured in the newspaper. The other two were unmasked in the wake of the "Shop a Yob" campaign. The *Mirror* continued its search for other hooligans as scores of readers contacted the hotline. Sean Knighton was pictured before and after donning a balaclava where he made a shooting gesture. He was sent home from the Sunderland tax office where he worked. Meanwhile, Vinny Jones apologized for biting the nose of *Mirror* reporter Ted Oliver. Businessman Graham McNulty, 38, from Hatherley in Cheltenham, was caught on camera hurling a plank. He was given a life ban by Aston Villa. The diehard fan and three others identified by the club received letters outlawing them from any future matches. After the riots in Malmö, he had been charged with beating up a policeman but cleared for lack of evidence, and advised not to return to Sweden. In TV footage of the Dublin match, the big, aggressive man – as he was described – was shown surrounded by thugs believed to belong to the far-right Cheltenham Volunteer Force. Unsurprisingly, many of the mothers of these men – shown on film to be hooligans – claimed that their sons were "good and decent" people who wouldn't harm anyone and had no connection to far-right groups. Three English yobs caged for their part in the Dublin riot bought their way out of jail and won their freedom when wealthy parents coughed up bail totalling £30,000. However, it was reported they could be back behind bars once they stood trial. Michael Williams, Andrew Hodges and Paul Kieser wept as an Irish High Court judge freed them. They had spent four nights in an isolated wing of Mountjoy prison and all three vowed they would return to face trial. They were facing serious charges, especially Williams and Hodges. Both were arrested after a nightclub doorman was beaten up and stabbed in the back, hours before the game. The victim needed 28 stitches and his injuries were life-threatening at one point.

On 28th February 1995, police feared that thugs involved in the Dublin riot would be heading for the Chelsea's European Cup Winners' Cup. Hooligans were reported to be planning to terrorize the Belgium city of Bruges. One Belgian police source told the *Mirror*: "We have been advised by officers in England that some of those involved in Dublin may be coming to our country. We have the names of a number of troublemakers allegedly involved in fighting two weeks ago. If they try to get into Belgium, we will arrest them and deport them." Police had already cracked down on drunken and ticketless fans arriving and had deported 140. Sixty-three hooligans were held after committing public order offences in Ostend and Bruges. The sinister riot-mob menace came just two weeks after the shameful events at Lansdowne Road, and one ferry skipper refused to take any fans unless they were handcuffed for the whole journey. Knives and tear gas were then confiscated. British and Belgium police were worried that around 800 fans – without tickets – would try to get into the match. A warehouse and a disused women's prison were set up as temporary holding cells for rioting thugs. Water canons were on standby, dogs were brought in and all police leave in the town was cancelled. More than 1,700 Chelsea supporters descended on Bruges, but fans had already ignored Glenn Hoddle's plea for peace and began running riot. Chelsea, however, expected few problems from their official party of 2,100 fans, who travelled under strict restrictions. However, the trouble got much worse.

The terrified citizens of Bruges were already counting the cost of British hooliganism in late February as 5,000 Chelsea fans laid siege to the city known as the "Venice of the North". Worried bar owners planned to shut down long before the Cup Winners' Cup clash and some shopkeepers didn't even dare open their doors. Ten years after Heysel, which turned Belgium against English football fans forever, many feared that torrential rain would force the match to be delayed by 48 hours. Bar owner Erik Dumalin said: "Soccer should be abolished. It is not a sport any more. Almost everybody will be closed and this match is costing us all a lot of money. I've already turned away a number of English soccer fans. The only word they seem to know is 'beer'." The match at the Olympic stadium was an 18,000 sell-out and Chelsea were confident there would be no problems with the official supporters. However, the situation had been inflamed by the presence of nearly 2,000 Chelsea followers who obtained tickets – many for the wrong end of the ground – by other means. There were also rumours of 1,000 forgeries circulating the canal-riddled city as drunken fans poured into Bruges. It was a holiday week in northern Belgium for the Mardi Gras carnival, and bars and restaurants said the match was robbing them of valuable business. At the start, they had no option but to stay open for their regular clients and the influx of holidaymakers. All in Bruges felt that once the hooligans had come and gone, they would be left picking up the pieces and paying for the damage. Hoddle, meanwhile, said:

"I have appealed to the fans to go only if they have a ticket, or enjoy the game and make sure we all come back with our heads held high. But it's out of our hands once that whistle goes and we have to be professional enough to concentrate on the job." "Football will bite its nails today as the threat looms of mob violence from Eurotrash fans," wrote the *Mirror*. More than 100 supporters had already been deported, but 1,000 more were expected to arrive in the city on the day of the match. The FA, fearful of more trouble, had an observer in Bruges, where there were some 500 local police officers and 50 undercover British police, and a helicopter was to fly over the city to film any incidents that might take place. Sadly, this was now the face of football. Belgian Francis Beest called the *Mirror Sport* to say that the yobs were out and about. "Three hooligans were smashing windows first thing in the morning," he reported. "They appeared still drunk from the previous evening and they knocked my little daughter off her bike as she cycled to school. What are these people? They stood there laughing. When we complained to Chelsea, they said the fans were not their supporters." Police had already confiscated more knives, and one fan injured in fighting was in hospital while others were under arrest for being drunk and disorderly. The chief police commissioner of Bruges, Roger de Bree, told reporters that they fully expected the hooligans to be extreme right-wing thugs.

Mobile phones were the latest gadget in the hooligans' war on soccer. As Bruges waited in fear of an invasion of English thugs, Chelsea's chief executive, Colin Hutchinson, revealed the latest weapon of the football hooligan. Chelsea summoned former Police

Chief Inspector Alan Beek to investigate the crowd disturbance at Stamford Bridge involving Millwall – which, at the time, was still the subject of an FA inquiry. Hutchinson said: "it didn't take the ex-chief inspector long to discover that prior to the pitch invasion fans had used mobile phones to co-ordinate their activities. It serves to illustrate that these fans are politically motivated and organized."

"There's no doubt in my mind that they were using the mobile phone to orchestrate that pitch invasion. I would say they were not Chelsea fans because they were operating in the lower tier of the North Stand which is not members only. We are doing our best to identify them. We are going through the video evidence and numerous photographs in the press."

In March 1995, it was reported that a whining soccer thug was suing a jail over his time there – because the laundry soap powder was too hard on his delicate hands. Chris Keen, who had a string of convictions and was caged for violent disorder, claimed that the detergent was harsh on his skin and damaged his clothes. He was seeking £49 in damages against David Sherwood, governor of Highpoint prison in Stradishall, Suffolk. The low-risk jail was where Keen was sent at the start of a 21-month sentence for rioting when his hometown of Leighton Buzzard, in Bedfordshire, played Aldershot. The 28-year-old yob, who incited fans to hurl bricks at rivals, was jailed in July 1994. The judge at Luton Crown Court said: "It was an ugly scene and police were outnumbered. It was lucky no one was hurt." Keen, who was in breach of a suspended sentence for attacking police, had later been moved to the high-security Wandsworth jail. Keen had made various claims against jails before and all had failed.

1997 – Brian Reade, Hitting Where It Hurt

In an article published on 15th October 1997, journalist Brian Reade wrote: "I didn't see the sharp object that hit me, but I felt the gash in my scalp. It matted my hair with blood and left me dazed, staggering, and more frightened than I've ever been in my life." He was referring to 30th May 1984, when he was outside the Olympic stadium in Rome, being chased by a baying Italian mob after Liverpool had beaten Roma in the European Cup final.

Before the game, the Romans had felt guilty about the administrative cock-up that saw them staging Europe's most prestigious Cup final on their own pitch, so they promised the travelling fans "heaven" – free beer, free pizza, free music, free love. It never materialized. Instead, they gave fans hell, according to Reade. "With as much free hate as we could stomach," he remembers. "As we left the stadium, we were greeted by gangs of youths on scooters, scarves around their faces and knives glinting in their hands, circling us and lashing out at any available limb." Others broke up the paving stones and aimed them at anything English, he recalls. Loud, ugly voices cut through the Roman night and spoke of "death to English bastards". A friend of Reade's had a knife shoved into his guts, and he knew an elderly man who was kicked senseless in a subway. "But what loosened my bowels more than anything else was the look on a policeman's face when I staggered towards him and asked for help." He snarled, raised his baton and pushed Reade back towards the seething masses. "I approached another Roman in riot gear and saw pure hatred in his eyes." They weren't there to protect the innocent, wrote Reade, they were there to protect their own. To gain kudos by battering the head of an English hooligan. To show their machismo to a watching world. Modern-day gladiators subjugating Anglo-Saxon scum. In 1997, watching events at the same stadium, Reade's mind rewound 13 years.

"Now, I never sympathize with England fans. I have always viewed people intent on troublemaking, who wrap themselves in Union Jacks and chant 'Enger-land' through lager-soaked mouths, as attention-seeking cretins." At the time of writing, Reade saw some again. Inadequate morons who had decided to take a Saturday night off from battering a better-looking lad in a Croydon nightclub to flaunt their manhood abroad. Morons, said Reade, that deserved cold prison breakfast until they "break through puberty". But commentators focusing on those sad figures as they analysed yet another night of violence, were missing the point totally, according to Reade. He cited that something very different from what had gone on before happened in Rome in 1997. "The overwhelming body of fans following England were typical of the overwhelming body of people who now follow English club football. In age, temperament, attitude and gender, that body is radically different from a decade ago."

However, Reade claimed that the Italian police missed this completely because they didn't want to practise anything other than the thuggish art of zero tolerance. And, consequently, many thousands of decent, peace-loving British citizens had the right to take their case to the European Court of Human Rights, he stated. "Because no individual deserves to be treated like vermin by a professional police force at an entertainment event between two nations supposedly so close we want to have the same heads on our coins."

Something worried Reade deeply as he saw the faces of some of the young men who left the Olympic stadium after their beating. Back in 1984, he saw the same faces on Liverpool fans who walked away from the same ground feeling shocked, humiliated and angry. The following year, in 1985, Reade was at the Heysel stadium for the Liverpool v Juventus match. He said: "It only took the glint of those knives and Italian voices chanting 'English bastards' to light the blue touchpaper. This time, led by the usual inadequate morons, young men ran at the Italians with vengeance in their heads ..."

While Reade was clearly advocating that the trouble should stop, he also strongly wanted to make the point that the Italian police – who were renowned for telling their own tales of bravery – would have blood on their hands should anything further go wrong at games played in their country. Reade said: "And again, they will turn their back, because zero tolerance means zero responsibility and zero civilization."

1998 – British Football Yobs Named in an Attempt to Avoid Disaster

Twenty hooligans were named by the *Mirror* on 12th January 1998 as organizers of violence. However, police were powerless to stop the men from travelling to the World Cup in France where it was thought that the hooligans planned to wreck it. Because of a legal loophole even thugs who were under restriction orders could not be stopped from slipping across the Channel. British Football Intelligence chiefs and French security bosses were to begin secret talks in Paris to assess the threat. A *Mirror* investigation revealed that some of the country's worst football hooligans were planning their travel routes and collecting money for black-market tickets and expenses. Ringleaders in Tyneside, London, the Midlands and Thames Valley had set up private bank accounts. Some belonged to the notorious gangs who brought shame to the terraces in the 1980s. A frightening number were Special Branch targets because of their right-wing activities and links to the vicious race-hate organization Combat 18. But police could not stop them heading for the tournament. Since the Football Spectators Act in 1989, only a handful had been put under restriction orders. Just 10 orders were in force in January 1998, but none of the *Mirror's* rogues gallery were under one at the time. The orders aimed to stop troublemakers travelling to matches abroad by making them report to a police station on the day of the match overseas. However, Detective Inspector Peter Chapman, head of the National Criminal Intelligence Service hooligan unit, told the *Mirror*: "A known hooligan who is under a restriction order can be on his way to an England game with a black-market ticket and some foreign currency in his pocket and there is nothing we can do. By the time the order has been breached, because he has not reported at a police station, he could be on the terraces."

Police wanted all convicted hooligans to be placed under restriction orders backed by tougher powers of arrest. British detectives were getting intelligence about plans for clashes with rival fans at service stations on French motorways and at railway stations. Several flashpoints had been identified in southern France where England fans were likely to meet rivals from Holland, Italy and Denmark. The *Mirror* learned that one gang in the Midlands had discussed battle plans with the violent Ultras in Marseille, where England were to play their first match. The worst hooligans were expected to use any means – including bogus passports and identity papers – to get to France. A detective said: "The ringleaders get their kicks out of organizing violence. They co-ordinate attacks using mobile phones on the terraces." The matches would be watched live by millions and fans would be constantly on the move to venues across France. There was not much time to introduce effective legislation to stop the known hooligans from travelling to Paris. The Football Supporters' Association had joined police in demanding tougher laws. Chapman, who was due in Paris for security talks, said: "Restriction orders must be more widely used by the courts but also toughened up to cope with the worst troublemakers. We would argue strongly for an additional power to allow police to stop hooligans subject to restriction orders from travelling to a match if there is a strong suspicion that they intend to do so."

The hooligans included Matthew Osbury, 27, yob and right-wing extremist who was connected to a number of firms and had power bases in west London and Nottingham. He was jailed in 1995 for six months and played a crucial role in cementing the Oxford, Reading, Chelsea hooligan triangle. Also on the list was one of Britain's worst soccer hooligans, who had been in the thick of the rioting in Rome in 1997. Plasterer Ian Cockburn, 28, was a leading Chelsea Headhunter linked to Fascist outfit Combat 18. In the 1980s he was connected to Ku Klux Klan activities. He had previously been spotted during numerous riots and had been jailed in Norway in 1995. By 1998 he had changed his last name to Holloway to avoid detection.

Number three in the rogues gallery was Stuart Glass, the skinhead leader of the Chelsea Headhunters. He stood as a National Front candidate in 1980 and was considered to be a key Combat 18 organizer. Others included builder Matthew Pullen, 26, who was banned from his home team at Shrewsbury Town. He was jailed for four months following the violence at the 1990 World Cup. Terry Hosking, a Liverpool yob, was renowned for turning nasty after a drinking binge. He was at Heysel in 1985 and one of his best friends was convicted of manslaughter. The 33-year-old was known to host drinking bouts for dozens of football yobs at his home. Tony Covele, 37, had been a known football hooligan for almost 20 years. He was the Headhunters' general and was known as Silver. He had links with London criminals and a string of convictions. Ian Sim was a leading Headhunter and linked to the main ringleaders in Kent and west London. He was held when a West Ham fan was knifed, but the victim refused to testify and Sim was released. Jason Abberly was a veteran Chelsea Headhunter who became heavily involved with football's right-wing fanatics in the late 1970s. He joined Combat 18's west London cell and was expelled from Norway for organizing violence. Paul Dodd was a key player in Carlisle's Border City Firm and was – at the time – Britain's worst soccer thug. Dodd, 26, had more than 30 convictions and was banned from all UK stadia. He was involved in the Dublin riot and was a key player in the riot in Rome. Darren Wells was a lethal combination of football hooligan and Fascist thug. He was a prime mover with the Headhunters and made a fortune promoting neo-Nazi music across Europe. Terry Blackham was a Crystal Palace thug with more than 20 convictions. He had strong links to the British National Party as well as the outlawed Ulster Defence Association, and was a gunrunner for Belfast terrorists.

Steve Hickmott, 41, had convictions stretching back to 1974. He was jailed for eight years in 1987 but his conviction was later quashed. Mark Atkinson was a neo-Nazi connected to the Headhunters. He was involved in the Ku Klux Klan before switching his allegiance to another racist group, Combat 18. Skinhead Tony Burke was viewed by police as a key organizer of violence, an active loyalist and involved in one of the key firms on the travel scene. Simon Lawley was an ex-soldier and Wolves hooligan with right-wing leanings. He was well known in Fascist circles in the West Midlands and had links to the Chelsea Headhunters. Steve Thomas, known as Fatty Thomas and Barrels, was a leading face among the Arsenal Gooners. He was respected amongst yobs for his organizational skills. Jeromy Lindley was a Millwall supporter kicked out of Ireland for incitement to racial hatred after giving a Nazi salute. Neil Keilty headed a 30-strong mob of notorious Aston Villa yobs. The firm was among the two worst on the international hooliganism scene. Andy Frain – who had a previous restriction order banning him from overseas games and was also under a lifetime ban from Reading FC – was thought to be making travel arrangements for the World Cup. Neill Jones was joint leader of the Border Front but was also linked with Newcastle United hooligan outfit The Gremlins and Oldham yobs. He was expected to spearhead travel arrangements for the World Cup in France. All these men had convictions for hooliganism.

"I saw the poor bloke punched to the ground ... someone was trying to stem the blood with a Fulham scarf," read the headlines in the *Mirror* in March 1998. Soccer fan Matthew Fox was battered to death hours before celebrating his 25th birthday. Matthew died after rival supporters were let out of Gillingham's soccer ground at the same time, following a hate-filled clash between Fulham and Gillingham supporters. Eyewitness, Peter George, had seen one of the bloodiest incidents in a weekend of violence which recalled the dark days of the 1980s and led the FA to hint at bringing back crowd control fences. Supporters slammed the "appalling decision" at the end of the match to let all the fans go out at the same time.

Tragically, soccer fan Matthew was killed after this "crazy" decision. The young printer – due to celebrate his birthday later that day – was punched and kicked to death by a mob of thugs lying in ambush. Bottles and coins had been thrown during the clash between Kentish side Gillingham and Fulham. For years there had been "bad blood" between supporters of the two clubs. Away fans were only separated from rivals by a fence and a line of policemen. And there was amazement that they had all been allowed to leave Priestfield ground together. Fulham supporter Joe Sene, a driver for the *Mirror*, claimed officials ignored "pure hatred" between supporters. He said: "I've never seen such a bad feeling between the fans. You could see the aggression on people's faces. At the end, the atmosphere was very volatile. It was a crazy decision to let the two sets of fans out at the same time. Normally, away supporters have to wait a while before leaving. But we were let out early. I thought to myself there was going to be trouble – and sure enough there was."

Gillingham supporter Terry Mulqueen, 55 said: "The police should have kept the Fulham supporters in the ground until the Gillingham fans were well clear. If there's trouble during a match, and then 10,500 people all leave at the same time, there's bound to be a problem." A spokeswoman for Fulham Supporters' Club said: "It should never have been allowed to happen."

Matthew's death was the most savage incident in a weekend of shocking soccer violence. Two episodes, which came just 10 weeks before the start of the World Cup in France, outraged FA bosses and recalled the grim violence of the 1970s and 1980s. They could even have hit England's campaign to host the 2006 World Cup. FA spokesman Steve Double warned that fences could go back up to stop supporters rushing onto the pitch. He said: "We don't want them back and at the moment it's not an option. But you can never say never." The pens were withdrawn after the Hillsborough disaster in which 96 people died.

Sports Minister Tony Banks launched a probe into policing at the death match. The FA also promised a probe. Tension had mounted inside the Priestfield ground after Gillingham scored the second goal of their 2-0 win in the 90th minute. The minute the ball hit the net, both sets of supporters surged towards a metal fence partition and started chanting at each other. Minutes later, the gates were opened and the fans poured out. A small number charged 40 yards down a three-foot alleyway at the bottom of Linden Road. There, they clashed with Gillingham supporters emerging out of the main home supporters' exit. Peter George, 49, of Romford, Essex, told how he saw Matthew beaten by his thug attackers. He said: "It was pandemonium. I saw one guy hit another bloke over the head with a sock full of coins.

"Then I saw this guy get punched and kicked to the ground by three or four others. The poor bloke was face down. One of his pals was trying to stop the flow of blood with his Fulham scarf. He was going berserk, screaming and shouting for help." Another witness, Giovanni Lanini, 28, saw Matthew's pals try to save him with heart massage and the kiss of life. He said: "One was shouting 'Foxy, get up!' Another was shouting, 'Why did it have to be like this?'" Julia Blackmore, 36, said: "A friend of the dead man was absolutely frantic. He was swearing hysterically and hitting himself about the face. He even started kicking a car." Alan Salmon, 49, stepfather of Matthew's close friend, Gary Preston, 27, told how his son had watched Matthew slump to the ground. He said: "Matthew was such a cheerful, jokey lad. He was so full of life. The people who have done this are from another planet." Matthew's family, from Purley, Surrey (now part of Greater London), were devastated. His parents, Ian, 50, and Pam, were "absolutely distraught". Matthew's cousin, Chris Baker, 40, said: "It was Matt's 25th birthday this Tuesday and they were holding a big family party for him on Saturday night. Now they're arranging his funeral. All he did was go to a match and he ends up coming home in a box. He was so full of life and had a great sense of humour."

Matthew was well known at Fulham where supporters' club official Anna Monks called him the club's "No. 1 fan". She said: "He was known to everyone, because he went to every match. Nobody should die over a game of football. There's been a history of problems between the two clubs. In 1995, Fulham and Gillingham fans were embroiled in a mass brawl on the pitch and one player suffered a broken leg. The animosity has remained."

About 60 police were at the game, which was not graded as one of the matches most likely to spark trouble. Gillingham chairman Paul Scally said: "Representatives of the FA and Football Licensing Authority both said the game was professionally stewarded and policed. We just had a nightmare scenario in which we scored on 90 minutes and the mood of the Fulham fans changed. We are devastated. It's desperately sad." Fulham manager Ray Wilkins said: "Our sympathy goes out to the young man's family." Three people were quizzed soon afterwards about Matthew's death, while police studied video footage.

Jack Straw, home secretary, was amongst the nearly 80,000 English fans who travelled to Wembley for the Coca-Cola Cup final between Chelsea and Middlesbrough. He stated: "It was a magnificent occasion which brought credit to the English game as a whole." It was the image of English football that he wanted to see at the World Cup in France, which was to take place in the summer of 1998. It was also the image which he felt would help England win the right to host the World Cup in 2006. "We cannot allow a small minority of thugs and hooligans to besmirch our game. The events of Saturday both at Gillingham and Barnsley, were shocking, and brought back memories of a dreadful past." Straw stated that his sympathies were with the family and friends of Matthew. He said: "Such events are, thankfully, rare at our football grounds. But we must be vigilant. Last week, I launched a campaign to ensure a peaceful and enjoyable World Cup for all decent fans. We are working closely with our French colleagues. They will welcome with open arms the respectable, law-abiding fan with tickets, but will come down hard on the hooligan. In doing so, they will have my firm support."

Straw continued, in a short article in the *Mirror*, by saying that all that could be done was being done to deter hooligans in Britain. A new hooligan hotline had been set up to help the "decent fan" fight back against the thugs by providing information to the police. Of the decent fans he said: "They are the lifeblood of our game and should be encouraged at every turn."

Ex-Fulham chairman, Jimmy Hill, said: "Like every decent person, I was shocked and horrified when the news came through that a Fulham supporter had died. I was already aware of the sickening happenings which took place at Barnsley. On top of that, to learn that a Rugby League referee had been attacked by fans was enough to make me wonder if an unknown foreign power had released an 'insanity' gas on England.

"In the memory of this unlucky young man, our inescapable duty is to unearth the reasons that caused the tragedy. It may well not be difficult to find fault with the precautions taken by the Gillingham Club, knowing of the bitter feelings which existed in the past between the players and supporters of both clubs. But football is a team game within clubs and has to be a team game among clubs, otherwise there is no one to play.

"If the loss of that young life enables this nation to awaken to the appalling levels of behaviour to which it has sunk, then it will not have been in vain. Blame Gillingham if you like for not employing more police and stewards. You can blame football for harbouring hooligans and for the indiscipline of too many of its players. Since religions have become unfashionable there is no recognisable code of decency.

"But in the meantime, don't expect forgiveness from FIFA. The FA should save the money being spent on the campaign to host the World Cup 2006. Unless we get the nation's house in order first, football will be the convenient martyr."

On the Saturday that Matthew died, at 3.40pm a near riot at the Barnsley versus Liverpool game came after referee Gary Willard sent off three Barnsley players. Play was suspended for four minutes and players grappled with fans on the pitch. At the exact same time, Everton stewards at Goodison Park stopped a crazed fan charging towards referee Neale Barry. The yob invaded the pitch during Everton's 4-1 defeat by Aston Villa. Just 35 minutes later, a Rugby League fan charged onto the pitch and knocked referee Stuart Cummings to the ground after he blew the final whistle to signal Sheffield Eagles' dramatic 22-18 win over Salford. One hour later, at 5.15pm, Matthew Fox was murdered after 50 fans fought a running battle outside the Priestfield stadium.

On 16th June 1998, soccer thug James Shayler's mother branded him "a sick yobbo". Stunned Maurecia saw the "Pig of Marseille" rioting on television but didn't realize the chunky lout was her own son. "I saw this yobbo running around in his shorts and told my husband they should be banned from every match. Little did I know it was my son." Father of three Shayler, 32, was jailed for two months after the *Mirror* pictured him leading rioters. The diehard Leeds United fan was hit with another blow when the club banned him from their ground for life. Shockingly, Shayler was a member of the English Supporters' Association and bought his ticket for the England v Tunisia game through the FA. He passed the vetting procedures despite having convictions for violence because they weren't related to football. A police source admitted that Shayler would not be known to the football unit of the National Criminal Intelligence Service. She said: "He definitely was not a category C (known hooligan). If he has never committed any football-related violence then he is not going to be on our database." Shayler's mum said: "I can't believe James. I've never seen this side before. I knew he had a Leeds United and a Yorkshire rose tattoo on his arm but I didn't know about the England flag on his tummy … He still comes home to watch Leeds play. Sometimes he takes his daughter Danielle. But whatever I think about him you can't get away from the pictures on the telly. I don't know what I'll say to him when I see him. I'll just want to know what happened. The only thing I can think of is that drink has caused all this trouble." She stated that James wasn't a big drinker and during the week he rarely went out. Most of the time, she said, he'll just have three pints of lager and that was his limit. She said that James' partner, Maria, was just as shocked as she was. One of Shayler's friends insisted that he was a decent family man who had been badly treated by the French and British authorities. The friend, who refused to give his name, said: "We're disgusted. His family has not been contacted by anyone in France. We don't know why the guy has been charged. We have not heard from the British Embassy. I phoned them, but they wouldn't tell me anything. If the guy has done something wrong that's one thing, but it doesn't matter what country you are in, you are entitled to a fair hearing. I don't know him as a violent bloke. He has been portrayed as a Class C hooligan."

However, Northants police said that Shayler was well known to them and that he had a number of spent convictions. Sports Minister Tony Banks said the FA would be investigating how Shayler, who joined the England Supporters' Association in April 1997, slipped through the net. The police source admitted that someone would be on the NCIS database if they attacked a fan at a football ground, but not if the attack happened in a pub. FA spokesman Steve Double said: "He will obviously be expelled immediately." Leeds Utd club chairman, Peter Ridsdale, said: "As a result of his behaviour in France we have banned him for life from Elland Road and from ever buying away tickets. We hope this sends a clear message to the mindless minority of thugs."

Two other ringleaders of the Marseille rioting were each jailed for four months in France. Known yobs Liam Yeomans – classified by police in Britain as a category C "extremely dangerous" hooligan – and Mark Thompson were also banned from returning to France for two years. Thompson was labelled as a category B "dangerous" hooligan. A third man, Paul Grover, got two months and was barred from France for one year. Skinhead Yeomans, 26, was told by Judge Jacqueline Faglin in Marseille: "You were there at the start of the violence on Sunday. You threw bottles and glasses at the police. You were one of the main agitators. You are well known in Britain. The British police warned us you were here." Yeomans, a tiler from Leicester, admitted being one of the first to hurl missiles at riot cops. Railwayman Thompson, 31, from Nuneaton, Warwicks, was told by the judge: "You threw bottles of beer at Tunisian supporters and police ... You were arrested outside the stadium on Monday while fighting with Tunisians after a police office recognized you from the previous evening." Thompson, a contract worker, was in France with four friends from the Midlands. The men showed no emotion as they were led off to the city's notorious Les Baumettes prison. They would join three other hooligans sent to prison, including the "Pig of Marseille" James Shayler. Grover was found guilty of attacking police outside the Velodrome stadium before the match against Tunisia. Grover, of Hanworth, west London, denied throwing glasses and bottles. Four more Britons would spend the rest of the World Cup in a prison cell before being brought before a judge on 15th July 1998. Shane Radford, 22, from London, Alan Libbiard, 28, a postman in the capital, and salesman Stephen Powell, 25, from Humberside, all denied throwing missiles at the police. Powell was also accused of brawling outside the stadium. He was arrested and identified in a police station by an Arab he allegedly attacked the day before. The fourth man remanded, Martin Kerr, 29, of Portsmouth, was charged with throwing cans of beer at police and resisting arrest. Dressed in an England kit, he told the judge he was on holiday with his wife and six-year-old child. He claimed he was knocked to the ground by Tunisians at the stadium and then arrested by a riot cop he thought was another fan.

Tensions rose, however, when more than half the supporters arrested during the Marseille riots were freed. In a shock move, 25 yobs were released from their cells and told to go where they pleased – including to England's other matches. British police and Home Office officials condemned the decision, saying it sent out a "dangerous message". Hundreds of England supporters began a mass exodus from Marseille and police feared many were heading for Montpellier – where Italy were to play Cameroon – where it was feared that revenge for the previous year's riots in Rome would be taken. Thousands more from the England camp headed for Toulouse for the next game against Romania. FIFA called on the British Government to step up efforts to stop hooligans going abroad. Spokesman Keith Cooper said: "We are not a police organization, we don't control frontiers. But we would like to see measures taken to prevent troublemakers from leaving their country at the time of important football competitions elsewhere." Senior officials in Marseille were calling for financial compensation for riot damage. And French Interior Minister Jean-Pierre Chevènement warned of tougher tactics against English thugs. He said: "No excuses will be tolerated." Other hooligans shamed by the *Mirror* included Cameron Campbell, a stripper in seedy clubs who was booted out of Watford Football Club due to his violence; Mark Woollett, a Millwall fan from Tonbridge, Kent; train driver Clem Ward, who was seen pointing a mock rifle and Ben Sharpe who, like Ward, was from Deeping St James in Lincolnshire.

Towards the end of June 1998, England soccer fans danced and sang in the streets of Toulouse while hundreds of German thugs went on the rampage in Lens. The tale of two World Cup cities spotlighted the security nightmare facing French police on flashpoint alert. In the southern city of Toulouse, where an army of English fans had gathered for the match against Romania on 22nd June, there was no repeat of the battle in Marseille. Supporters enjoyed a carnival atmosphere in the brilliant sunshine – determined to show the world the smiling face of English football. One of Toulouse's leading regional newspapers, *La Dépêche*, reported: "The English have arrived and happily the town has not been taken over by psychosis, even if a lot of people will be staying at home." However, the newspaper went on to describe the hooligans that were present and claimed that disorder could have broken out at any moment. Nevertheless, it reported it was confident in the forces of the law who had worked hard to prepare for any trouble. "It is a weekend of risk, but there is no fear in the town. The people of Toulouse have realized that not all England fans are hooligans."

However, in the northern mining town of Lens, 96 hooligans were arrested in running battles with police, which left one officer in a coma and a journalist seriously injured. The violence flared before Germany's drawn game with Yugoslavia. The 1,000-strong mob of rioters was described by a senior officer as "sober, organized, mobile thugs using communications to disperse and regroup rapidly". The injured policeman – Daniel Nivel, 43, from Arres, who was married with two children – was hit on the back of the head with an iron bar. He was flown by helicopter to nearby Lille where he was found to be in a serious condition. A Brazilian TV journalist was smashed to the ground by German thugs who left him for dead. Colleague Roberta Silva, who worked for the Globo TV station, said later: "A group of about 10 to 20 Germans jumped on him and beat him to the ground. They tried to grab the camera and I tried to stop them but then they smashed it as well."

Back in Toulouse, it was discovered that banned World Cup penknives were on sale just hours before England's match with Romania. The four-inch blades were withdrawn after PM Tony Blair protested that thugs could use them as weapons. But the *Mirror* found boxes of them openly on sale at the main railway station in Toulouse, where thousands of English fans arrived for the match. The manager of Relais H newsagents claimed he had no idea they were banned. He merely shrugged his shoulders and said he had no plans to withdrawn them from sale. But FA spokesman Steve Double said: "this gives out the wrong message. We understand they had been banned and we will be asking the authorities why this appears not to have happened."

Back in Lens, the unnamed cameraman was taken to hospital unconscious. Police chief Daniel Cadous said: "There were a lot of incidents after the match. Several hundred German hooligans moved in and started smashing and tearing down the perimeter security fencing. It was not like in Marseille where the supporters were drunk." Meanwhile, the sun finally shone on English football in Toulouse. Happy fans kicked a ball around with the locals and joked with passersby, some were even kissing. In the shadow of the magnificent Stadium Municipal, hundreds dived into a huge open-air swimming pool, with French families joining in the fun. By late afternoon, the bars in the city's two main squares were packed with chanting supporters enjoying themselves in the sweltering heat. In the pretty Place de Wilson, they cooled off in fountains as temperatures hit the 90s. Bar owners had feared the worst. But Allouch Marcel, 54, manager of the Brasserie les Arcades on Capitol Square, was full of praise for the England fans. He said: "We've been worrying for the last few days, but they couldn't have been more respectful. They've been chanting football songs outside my bar all day and the whole thing has been good-natured and friendly." Other bar owners, including English bar owners, said that they hadn't had to throw one fan out, and some even went so far as to say that the fans were the friendliest that they'd had in Toulouse for 14 years. There hadn't been any problems for almost a week – ever since the fans started arriving for the match in the city. Many campsites played host to fans from different countries and there hadn't been any trouble there either. However, just in case, an extra

1,600 police officers were drafted in to Toulouse. Riot cops waited in vans but did not spoil the party mood.

In Lens, British intelligence officers feared that Nazi-styled louts would head for the town for a showdown with England supporters before the forthcoming match with Colombia. There were also fears for the safety of Prince Harry who was due to be at the match with Prince Charles, despite warnings by British Embassy officials of the riot danger.

In another move, the French revealed that they had in place a tough new crackdown on English and Scottish fans, which allowed them to kick out "several hundred" category C hooligans as soon as they were spotted. The emergency powers followed a meeting between French police chiefs and Detective Inspector Peter Chapman, head of the National Criminal Intelligence Service football unit. Home Secretary Jack Straw said: "I am sure all genuine supporters will welcome this move. The French are sending out a clear message that thugs are not welcome and will not be allowed to spoil the tournament." An NCIS spokesman said: "We want to make any hooligans who are thinking of coming to the World Cup and causing trouble to think again." One known English football hooligan with a history of violence was immediately sent home when he arrived in Paris on a Eurostar train from Waterloo. Authorities claimed Martin Townsend, 35, from the Manchester area, was one of the most serious category C hooligans, and was headed for Toulouse to cause trouble at the England–Romania match. Four suspected England soccer hooligans were also arrested in Toulouse.

It was reported exactly what had happened to innocent police officer Daniel Nivel. "A German soccer thug batters an iron bar on the head of a helpless cop," said the newspapers. It was the sickening moment when the policeman was sent into a deep, life-threatening coma.

Doctors said the 43-year-old father – who was on life support – was suffering from irreversible brain damage. In the aftermath of the attack, Germany struggled to come to terms with its shame for the worst scenes of violence at the World Cup up to this time. Nivel was ambushed by a 50-strong gang after 650 hard-core German hooligans went on the rampage in Lens. As the gang swept down the road, they yelled: "We are Germans! We're scared of nothing. Let's get the cops!" Faced with the onslaught, two police took to their heels, but Nivel stood his ground. One thug smashed the cop's gun in two and battered him with the butt. Another beat his with a beer bottle. A third bludgeoned him with a wooden advertising sign. And a fourth pounded at him with the iron bar. A skinhead, Markus Warnecke, 27, from Hanover, was in custody after being charged with the attack. One of the gang said: "Everybody kicked him. They behaved like beasts."

A picture of the "vicious" German was published in the *Mirror*. Readers were told he had taken the French policeman to the brink of death. The newspapers also published the shocking pictures of Nivel being attacked, being beaten with an iron bar and left lying in a pool of blood as his cowardly attackers then dashed for safety. A shaken Germany was suffering the same shame as England had done many times before. Warnecke – usually dressed in a T-shirt with the word Pitbull across the front – belonged to a skinhead gang called Bones. He was one of the 650 category C soccer hooligans from Germany who fought after Germany's 2-2 draw with Yugoslavia. Police said the lout ran a tattoo studio in Hanover, and had a string of convictions for assault and carrying a weapon. The hooligan faced years in jail. He was being held along with fellow German, Karl-Heinz Elschner, over the attack on Nivel. They and others were interviewed by police, and a 17-year-old told how he had gone on the rampage with the right-wing extremists. He said: "There were 50 of us, the hard core, marching through the city centre, shouting. Anybody who wasn't German got thumped. About 150 French fans were scared as hell and took cover behind the cops. We went into a side road where there were three police by themselves. We shouted at them … The police yelled back in French and then the cops got scared. Two ran away. The third wanted to load his gun, but we grabbed him. I saw one bloke smash the gun and two batter the policeman with the butt. Another gave him one with a beer bottle and somebody else hit him on the head with a wooden advertising sign. Everybody kicked him. They behaved like beasts. Then I ran away." The thugs came from the north German cities of Hamburg and Hanover and appeared to have been organized by a ringleader known as the Boss. He was identified in Germany as Torsten W, a well-known troublemaker at Hamburg SV. Another thug was named as the owner of a brothel in Hamburg's red light district, the Reeperbahn. Yet another was identified as a Greek locksmith with a long history of violence in the Hamburg area. Only 50 of the louts had tickets – the rest watched the match in local cafés. Worried police believed the trouble was planned and orchestrated for political ends. The soccer thugs were reported to have growing links to the spawning neo-Nazi gangs causing massive problems in Germany. Many of the thugs chanted right-wing abuse, yet they were completely sober and fairly smartly dressed. The *Frankfurter Allgemeine* – Germany's equivalent of *The Times* – said: "It seems these are coolly-calculating neo-Nazis using modern means of technology to further their aims." Another paper added: "The Brazilians dance the samba and the Jamaicans have a party. But hordes of Germans shouting 'Sieg … Sieg' seem like a military formation." Some experts argued that there was no evidence that the soccer thugs were becoming politicized, but one admitted: "Raising Nazi salutes and shouting racist slogans is seen to be cool."

The bloody riot by the so-called fans threatened Germany's bid to stage the 2006 World Cup. But, for Germans, even more worrying were fears of the continuing rise of the neo-Nazi sympathizers and the resulting escalating violence. A Government report estimated that the number of far-right extremists in Germany grew to 48,400 in 1997 – a leap of 7 per cent. The number of neo-Nazis prepared to carry out violent acts soared by almost 20 per cent to 7,600. As evidence, mini-arsenals were discovered throughout the country. A raid on one house in the Saar revealed makeshift bombs, an anti-tank weapon and pump-guns.

In Britain, the Government was considering confiscating the passports of convicted football yobs via the courts. Home Office minister, Alun Michael, said: "The withdrawal of passport facilities would be a very serious step. But we will give consideration to it." One incident involved an English fan, who was reported to be in a serious condition after he was knifed in the stomach. Toulouse police said that Steven Clarke from Stourbridge, West Midlands, was an innocent bystander. Soccer thug Maurice Woodward, who was involved in the Marseille riots, was jailed for four months. Builder Woodward, 25, from Rotherham, South Yorks, was caught on video throwing bottles. He was rated a category C thug. Meanwhile Terrence Yems, 35, from Epson, Surrey, was given a two-month suspended sentence for stealing tickets from a fan in Toulouse.

Back in Lens, there was a 30-mile booze exclusion zone planned for England's game against Columbia. It was clear that Germany's emerging army of neo-Nazis fuelled the violence on the streets of Lens. They were among the hundreds of fans who battled with police, giving Hitler salutes and chanting racist slogans. Experts were convinced the violence was too well organized for the fighting to be spontaneous. The French authorities were desperate to find out how big a role the neo-Nazis played. The World Cup was the perfect stage for Germany's new generation of "ultra-right-wing thugs" to grab the headlines. Extremism was thriving on the economic mayhem caused by the reunification of East and West Germany. There were chilling parallels to the mass unemployment and street violence of the 1930s, which had swept Hitler to power. On some scarred housing estates in the former East Germany as many as half of the men were jobless – and anger was rising, according to newspaper reports. Neo-Nazi activitists were moving in to take advantage. They were going door to door "spreading an evil message", according to the *Mirror*.

The "chaoten", as they were dubbed, had formed dozens of

gangs based on soccer and violence. They included the North Side Boyz, who supported FC Cologne, and Chevignon Fighters in Düsseldorf. The violence seen in Lens was commonplace in many German cities at the time. Foreigners were regularly ambushed, beaten and even murdered – homes were attacked and often burned. Right-wing extremists also were winning support at the polls. Two months prior to Lens, neo-Nazis grabbed 12 per cent of the vote in the ex-eastern state of Saxony-Anhalt, their highest since the Second World War. Sociology professor Günter Pilz warned: "There was a dangerous mix of neo-Nazis and frustrated, ticketless fans in Lens. Only a massive police presence will stop it happening again." He said the thugs were a social melting pot: "Lawyers and middle-class people are dressing cheaply and mingling with the mob. Many don't belong to an organization. They regard rioting as a hobby." Frankfurt police chief, Heiko Homolia, said: "Our hooligans are a tightly organized body. Ringleaders arrange meetings by the internet, they fax plans to each other and strike with the speed of lightning. The leaders hardly touch alcohol before violence and it is hard to recognize them as hooligans. Any expert could have foreseen trouble in Lens. Practically every one of the 3,000 or so German hooligans is known to us." French police were alarmed to find internet messages calling on Germans to cause trouble.

Before the Chile v Cameroon match, two German neo-Nazis carrying baseball bats were arrested. Security bosses had mobilized extra riot police for Germany's game in Montpelier with Iran. The events in Lens had lifted the lid and shown the world the violent forces stirring inside modern Germany. The rabble, now roused, were about to make Europe a dangerous place.

On 4th July 1998, an England fan confessed to stabbing a Frenchman to death after mistaking him for an Argentinean. Paul Birch, 43, told police his victim had "smirked" at him on the night of England's World Cup defeat by Argentina. The pair were fellow passengers on a rail journey from Grenoble to Lyon and the Frenchman, Eric Frachet, 33, was knifed in the stomach when the train stopped at the tiny country station of Saint-André-le-Gaz. Birch, an engineer from London, ran from the scene after dodging rail staff. He was held the following night in Grenoble after police were called to investigate a bust-up at a hotel. Birch had picked a fight with a nightwatchman.

Detectives said that while being quizzed over that incident he confessed to the stabbing of Frachet. He was remanded in custody and charged with murder. Police said: "He told detectives he was travelling on a train when he saw the man sitting opposite was smirking. He said he guessed he was an Argentinean who was mocking him, so he waited until the train pulled into the next station then stabbed him and ran off." It then emerged that Frachet was a mild-mannered man with no interest in football. He was a struggling actor on his way to Paris to audition for a TV commercial. The stabbing happened at about kick-off time in England's last-16 match with Argentina in Saint-Étienne, which they lost on penalties. Birch, reported to be a divorced father of two, was not known to police as a football hooligan. He was in France for the World Cup and saw England play Colombia in Lens.

Birch ended up being examined by a psychiatrist because of

his strange behaviour since his arrest. A police spokesman said he would remain in custody until a trial date was set. Public prosecutor Xavier Bonpain said Birch "did not appear to have all his marbles". He confirmed that authorities had requested psychiatric reports and more information from England. The prosecutor said: "His behaviour has been very strange." Mr Frachet, who lived alone near Grenoble, died on the way to hospital. He suffered massive blood loss from a three-inch deep wound. The victim's friends were heartbroken. He was described as a "gentle, funny, intelligent man". Close friend Dominique Biernaux said: "He was clever, witty and hard-working. The last thing he would do is provoke an English football fan into attacking him. He just wasn't that kind of man. He didn't even like football. If you sat opposite him on a train, he would probably barely look up at you, let alone pull faces. He was taking a train to Paris that night for an audition for a television commercial the next day. He wasn't a well-known actor but he had been seen on television adverts now and again and had had some success in local theatres."

Despite all the horrific incidents that happened during the World Cup, football thugs who went on the rampage were free to do it again after plans to hit them with a travel ban collapsed in chaos. The pledges of tough action had seen just 30 hooligans put on restriction orders to stop them going to overseas games, the Home Office admitted in August 1998. Police chiefs and MPs feared the yobs could wreck the qualifying games for Euro 2000. Hundreds of known hooligans who headed for the World Cup escaped the threat of a ban because the French authorities jailed just 20. Another 11 were on bail or awaiting trial, but many of them insisted they were innocent. The low number of convictions meant that Home Secretary Jack Straw was powerless to act against the vast bulk of identified troublemakers. Travel restrictions and entry bans to soccer grounds could be imposed only against thugs found guilty of crimes. French police arrested 275 hooligans during the World Cup and stopped another 363 suspected thugs entering the country. Only a fraction were taken to court, and 14 were expelled from the country. Furious MPs accused the French authorities of a "slap on the wrist" approach, which left hooligans free to plot future riots.

James Shayler, meanwhile, was back behind bars in August 1998, having been freed from prison in France. The man who shamed England during the Marseille riots was facing drugs charges in Britain. He was arrested by police after landing at Gatwick. He was due before magistrates at Wellingborough in Northamptonshire on charges of conspiracy to supply drugs. The beer-bellied thug had been jailed for two months in France.

In October 1998, a girl soccer thug at the centre of a riot that wrecked a city centre was still being hunted by police – five months after the riot. More than 500 drunken fans gathered in Newcastle's Bigg Market after Newcastle United's FA Cup final defeat by Arsenal in May that year. The woman was filmed encouraging a yob to smash a phone box. Then she climbed on it half-naked. The police issued a picture of the woman they claimed was involved and some of another 17 people still wanted over the riot. A police spokesman said: "They brought shame on the city. Many are easily identifiable from the photographs." Eight people were arrested at the time for drunkenness and public order offences.

1999 – Soccer Movie Murder Link

A soccer fan, Keith Hargreaves, who battered a man to death after watching a violent film about football hooliganism, was jailed for life on 7th July 1999.

Keith's son, Richard, also got life for killing 46-year-old Terrence Smalley after a row. Millwall fan Keith Hargreaves, 46, who was babysitting at his daughter's home, told the Old Bailey that the 1995 soccer film *ID* got him so worked up he got out a baseball bat. He said he waved it around his head as he joined in a chant from the film about attacking rival fans with baseball bats. He said: "I was like a 17-year-old again. The film reminded me of the old days at Millwall as if it was only yesterday." Later that night, he and Richard rowed with drunken Smalley and battered him to death with the bat. Smalley was also slashed with a meat cleaver in the flat in Dulwich, south London.

In November that year, a crazed World Cup football thug who screamed "it's a knockout", as he beat a French policeman into a coma was jailed for 10 years. Daniel Nivel, 43, suffered brain damage in the savage attack by Andre Zawacki and three other German neo-Nazis, leaving him blind in one eye and barely able to speak. The French officer was in court in Essen, Germany, as the men were convicted. Judge Rudolf Esders told them: "You are not monsters but you behaved like monsters on that day." Zawacki, 28, who smashed Mr Nivel's skull with the butt of his tear-gas launcher, was convicted of attempted murder. Tobias Reifschlaeger was given six years. Frank Renger got five years and Christopher Rauch, 24, three-and-a-half years for the assault in Lens, France, in June 1998. Reifschlaeger, 25, and Renger, 31, apologized to Mr Nivel during the seven-month case and called for an end to all football violence. Outside court, Mr Nivel's son, Vincent, 17, said: "I can never forgive them."

Just one month later, a soccer thug who was captured on TV waving a Nazi flag and organizing fights was sacked from his job on 11th November 1999. Jason Marriner, 32, a ringleader of the notorious Chelsea Headhunters, was fired by a London tyre firm after millions of BBC viewers saw him bragging about his violent exploits. Tattooed Marriner was seen laughing as he reduced a Polish visitor to tears boasting about how he had climbed into one of the gas chambers at Auschwitz. Andy Frain, another Chelsea Headhunter, boasted to the camera that he had slashed a policeman's throat.

Reporter Donal MacIntyre, who spent a year filming the thugs for *MacIntyre Undercover*, screened in early November 1999, was forced into hiding after receiving three death threats. A colleague said: "Donal will be staying in a safe house. He knew these people were seriously into violence and they have very long memories. He has vowed never to go to a football match." Police asked the BBC for a tape of the show. Scotland Yard said: "We are aware of the contents and we will take the appropriate action." Marriner, who was seen with a Nazi flag at Chelsea's Copenhagen clash, was likely to have his season ticket confiscated. Frain, 35, told MacIntyre how he stabbed a policeman as he stopped off in Penrith, Cumbria, on the way to a match in Scotland in August 1991. One man was arrested and cleared after a trial. Fellow hooligans bombarded the TV thugs with abusive emails. A police intelligence source said: "The websites we monitor are full of messages blasting them for being so stupid. The hooligan fraternity is not pleased at the way they managed to stitch themselves up and drop other people in it."

Two men were arrested on 11th November 1999 in connection with an attack, allegedly by the Arsenal "Gooners" gang on a Manchester United fan in August 1999. Police had mounted a massive security operation in preparation for the England–Scotland match in Glasgow on 12th November. They feared that 40 of England's worst hooligans were planning to rendezvous in Carlisle.

2000 – UEFA's Complacency Brings Back Chilling Memories

In 2000 the *Mirror* said: "Déjà vu does not play in Chelsea's midfield but in the mind of every football fan whose memory stretches back further than Andy Gray's ability to draw white lines on screen." In fact, it was visions of Gray's fearless aggression which flooded back on 24th March 2000, as English club football returned to its true position as the powerhouse of the European game. The last time English sides struck such fear into the hearts of continental opponents was in May 1985. Gray's Everton tore Rapid Vienna apart in Rotterdam to win the Cup Winners' Cup, and a fortnight later Liverpool went to the Heysel stadium, clear favourites at the time, to beat Juventus and take the European Cup for the fifth time. But the events of that terrible match led to English clubs being banned from European competition for five years.

Football fans waited a decade before their teams wrestled back the superiority they'd had over the Italians, Germans and Spanish. That is why, the week before European results should have instilled English fans with a pride not seen for 15 years. However, something else was festering away in the background, which made the parallels with Belgium and 1985 far more worrying. The state of the Mambourg stadium in Charleroi, where England were to meet with Germany on 17th June 2000, was causing concern. Noises were being made by Belgian police and ground safety experts about the possibility of a second "Heysel". It was a risky venue, according to some experts. Dr Jim Dickie, a widely respected structural engineer, who was a safety consultant to several leading British clubs, was appalled by what he saw at the 30,000-seater stadium. The stairways were too wide, the railings too low and the exits too narrow. A third tier had been erected, which Dr Dickie said would not get a UK safety certificate. He said he would not attend the game if offered a ticket because "the levels of risk are unacceptably high".

The Belgian Police Federation was so worried that it demanded the game be switched to the King Baudouin stadium in Brussels (ironically, the site of the old Heysel stadium). Its chairman, Paul van Keer, said of the Charleroi ground: "It is totally unfit to deal with troublemakers and even the smallest problem could lead to tragedy." However, the UEFA suits waved away such protests and played the old turn about everything being alright on the night.

For the fans caught up in Heysel and Hillsborough disasters, such arrogance and indifference was chilling. A brief glance at the ticket allocation for potentially the most explosive game at Euro 2000 sent the chills into "permafreeze". Before the teams were known, 36 per cent of the tickets were sold to neutrals, some over the Internet. So how many black-market ticket touts had them was anybody's guess. When sponsors, media, UEFA and corporate hospitality had their tickets it left a mere 4,800 tickets for England fans and the same for the Germans. At an unsafe ground, a bottle-throw away from Dover and Düsseldorf, it presented a potential time bomb that was simply unacceptable. Both UEFA and the Belgian authorities had been charged with criminal neglect after Heysel. It appeared they were willing to risk charges again ...

The reason cited for their complete disregard for the advice given by experts was that they believed hooliganism was a distant evil. If that really was the case, then the *Mirror* suggested that all those involved were "unworthy of office". Racist chants were still being heard throughout stadiums every weekend. The *Mirror* said there is "a horrible feeling about this game because ... when football authorities insult the fans over ticket allocation and ignore the safety experts, they court disaster". Richard van Eijk, the Euro 2000 spokesman, said: "there is zero per cent chance of the England–Germany game being moved. There is no problem with the stadium at all." Reading those words, for those who knew better, filled them with "déjà vu ... and a dread these faceless officials will never be able to comprehend.

When it was possible that England might face Italy in Euro 2000 at the site of the Heysel disaster, Italy's footballers were told to order their families to stay away. They feared the mayhem being caused by England's hooligan fans. Their worries were heightened by the fact that there had been rioting in Charleroi and Brussels the previous weekend. However, it was also announced that England could be kicked out of Euro 2000 if there was any more trouble. If England drew with Romania, they would play Italy the following Saturday. Italian midfielder Luigi di Biagio said: "the hooligans represent a serious problem to the point where I would advise my family not to come to the match. I will not allow them to go to the stadium in Brussels because I could not play with the right frame of mind. It is better that they should stay inside the hotel. If there is anything to celebrate, it can be done the next day."

Defender Paolo Maldini added: "We are worried the Belgian police don't manage to contain them, even though it has been known for months there would be a situation of tension and danger." It was suggested that the potential quarter-final be moved from Brussels to Amsterdam. Meanwhile, Italian soccer chiefs and players had sympathy for the plight of the England team and the FA. In November 2000, two alleged football hooligans, said by a TV documentary to be part of the Chelsea Headhunter gang, faced court. Jason Marriner and Andrew Frain, were shown on the MacIntyre programme going to a game at Leicester to stir up trouble, the jury was told. Frain was caught by a secret camera, it was said, relishing the fear that would follow the news that he was "on the loose". Both denied conspiracy to commit violent disorder. They also pleaded not guilty to affray. Marriner's QC, Michael Wolkind, attacked reporter Donal MacIntyre and colleague Paul Atkinson by calling them "two dangerous men you cannot trust". They posed as criminals to try to impress Marriner. Mr Wolkind said the pair showed "smugness and arrogance" over their control of Marriner. The QC alleged that there was "misleading editing" in their film and "cuts out of sequence". One shot amounted to a "dirty, little lie". MacIntyre, he claimed, had used similar tactics when infiltrating a residential care home in Kent. The case continued.

2001 – Lout of Range

Police said they were winning the battle to stop English soccer thugs causing mayhem abroad. Ten thousand fans travelled to Germany for the World Cup match but just 78 were arrested. Small groups of hooligans hurled bottles and glasses as terrified shoppers fled in panic in Munich. Seventeen people, including 10 police officers, needed hospital treatment. But German and British police said the violence was not as bad as predicted. Ron Hogg, of the Association of Chief Police Officers, said: "Out of the 10,000 England fans in Munich, we believe there were just 300 who were involved in trouble. Those 300 are an absolute disgrace." Undercover intelligence officers had been compiling video and photo evidence to nab the hooligans who made it to Germany. Many were stopped before they could leave England. Some 565 fans were banned from going to the game under the Football Disorder Act brought in in 2000. Seventy-nine suspected troublemakers were stopped at ports and airports and told they could not leave the UK. Six fans appeared before a special court after an investigation into the Chelsea Headhunters gang. Anthony Covele, 41, Desmond O'Flynn, 36, Brian Mongey, 37, Anthony Dempsey, 31, Richard Boulter, 42, and Ray Kennedy, 30, were picked up at Heathrow airport and given conditional bail to appear in court at a later date. They were not allowed to attend any Chelsea or England matches.

A football thug arrested for going within two miles of a ground got off because police messed up the measurements – said the *Mirror*. They said the distance from the stadium car park to the pub where Carl Gough was nicked was 1.99 miles. But the charges were dropped after Gough's lawyer argued that the measurement should have been taken from the pitch's centre spot – a distance of more than two miles. Gough, 37, said: "they measured the distance from the top of the car park so they could get me within a two-mile radius of the ground. I didn't understand it. When I was at school a radius always started at the centre." His solicitor, Steve Cobley, said: "The charges were extremely unreasonable as he was nowhere near the ground." Gough, banned in October 2000 from going within two miles of any match in Derby, was arrested after being spotted in the Friargate pub in the city centre during England's clash with Mexico at nearby Pride Park. The hooligan, from Sandiacre, Derbyshire, was due to appear before Derby magistrates in July 2001 with breaking the banning order. But the Crown Prosecution Service agreed to drop the case. A spokeswoman said: "It was not felt that it would be in the public interest to continue to prosecute."

2002 – England v Poland and that's Just the Picture

A photograph of English football fans beating up their Polish counterparts in Warsaw was the first prize in the world's most bizarre pub quiz. The Kiels Hools gang from the Beerschot club in Antwerp, Belgium, invited gangs from Bruges and Groningen to a charity pub quiz about the history of football hooliganism. (Not surprisingly, anxious police stood by, fearing riots.) Amazingly, it was trouble-free and the evening raised £10,000 for medical treatment to help a four-year-old boy suffering with cancer.

In May 2002, shocked police told how they prevented the Millwall soccer riot turning into a fight to the death. They moved in to shepherd away a group of rival Birmingham City supporters who were "itching for a confrontation". Chief Superintendent Mike Humphrey said: "They didn't realize how serious it was. I don't think they appreciated that we were trying to save their lives." He described the riot as "sheer hell", and added: "There could easily have been a fatality." Following the rioting, it was mooted that police were considering suing Millwall FC and stopping patrolling its games after 900 fans went on the rampage in scenes of violence.

In disgraceful violence, recalling the worst days of soccer hooliganism, officers were pelted for more than an hour with paving stones, bricks, flares and thunderflashes. Two cars were set on fire and a children's playground trashed for ammunition. Forty-seven officers were hurt, with nine needing hospital treatment for injuries, including broken limbs. One officer, hit by flying concrete, needed seven stitches in his face. Twenty-six of 34 horses on duty were also hurt. Seven people were arrested. Humphrey, who led 250 police against the thugs, said his officers could have been killed. He said: "We had lots of men on the scene but weren't prepared for the ferocity and viciousness of the attack. It was far beyond anything we imagined. The hooligans were there to cause as much injury as they could. It was absolutely disgraceful. This is not a normal incident. This was toe-to-toe fighting and they weren't running away. It was sheer hell. Millwall has always been a difficult club, but last night it disgraced itself."

As officers fought with jeering hooligans others led Birmingham City fans to safety. In an unprecedented move, police planned to sue the south London club and the Football League for the cost of policing the riot. Outraged Deputy Commissioner Ian Blair said: "This is absolutely unacceptable. I'll be bringing Millwall and the Football League into Scotland Yard and shall take legal advice over whether it is appropriate to seek compensation. We had cars on fire, residents hiding in desperate fear and officers with broken legs and arms. Anybody should be asking what has gone on." Officers had to admit that they could no longer cope with the continuing violence at the troubled club and said the riot was the "last straw".

Scotland Yard threatened to withdraw the policing of matches – which costs hundreds of thousands of pounds – unless the club clamped down on its hooligans. Millwall police liaison officer, Neil MacPherson, told the BBC series, *Hooligans*: "We don't have the resources to do anything other than keep the lid on it." Reg Burr, president of the shamed club, said any of the rioters who could be named would be banned from the club for life. For 70 minutes the mob went berserk, ripping up paving stones from a nearby playground to throw at mounted officers. Missiles were thrown in volleys of up to 50 at a time. So many officers were injured a field hospital had to be set up in the club grounds, where they were treated by ambulance staff and the Millwall club doctor. One police horse, named Alamein, suffered serious injuries when a thunderflash exploded beneath the eight-year-old. The frightened animal reared and came smashing down through a car, severing an artery in its leg. It needed life-saving treatment from a specialist vet.

Heartbroken Steve Claridge told of his disgust at the mindless thugs who had taken the gloss off Millwall's remarkable season. The veteran striker was devastated when the south London side crashed out of the play-off semi-final, and he knew that whatever success that they enjoyed in the future would be overshadowed by the hooligans and their intent on shaming football. The *Mirror* published the pictures of 10 men wanted for the hooliganism at Millwall. Police released a total of 16 pictures from the mayhem and were determined to track down those responsible. Darren Finch, 27, pleaded guilty to violent disorder and was remanded in custody. John Parker, 18, was also in court and accused of affray. He did not make a plea and police continued to study the video evidence. James Mullen, 19, was also charged with affray. Both were released on bail. Seven people had appeared in court by 9th September 2002. A city worker was also accused of taking part in the rioting. He appeared at the Old Bailey. Ian Stone, 24, an employee of HSBC, was charged with violent disorder. John Manzarolli, 24, and 19-year-old Paul Healey appeared alongside Stone, accused of the same offence.

In May 2002, the world's most notorious soccer thug found himself free to travel to the World Cup after his early release from prison. German neo-Nazi Markus Warnecke was freed after three years – following the battering of French policeman Daniel Nivel – and was able to fly to Japan and Korea. Police said that Warnecke, who had a series of convictions for violence, would face no action unless there was any indication that he would commit violence. A spokesman in his hometown of Hildesheim said: "He does not have to check in with police." He was free to go to any football match he wanted to. As far as police were concerned, he had served his sentence and that was that. The fact that he was involved in the Nivel attack was not enough to constitute a threat. However, in Britain, a soccer thug dubbed England's No 1 hooligan was banned from going to the World Cup and every match in England and Wales. Carlisle United supporter Paul Dodd yawned as a judge imposed the six-year order on 19th May 2002. Dodd was due out of jail the following day after a sentence for taking part in trouble before a Carlisle–Hull City game. The order allowed police to seize his passport. Meanwhile, an England fan became the first to be kicked out of the World Cup. Derby County supporter Andrew Cooper, 37, was detained after arriving in South Korea and was expected to be sent home on the next available flight. Although not banned, Cooper was sentenced to four months in jail in 1999 for possessing CS gas. The Japanese and South Korean authorities were informed and he was advised against going. A total of 1,007 England hooligans were banned from tournaments.

A football hooligan who claimed to be "the baddest in Britain" was planning a £3,000 trip to the World Cup. Gang leader Gilroy Shaw, who featured in the BBC *Hooligans* programme, had been banned from matches for 11 of the past 14 years. But his banning order expired in 2002 – just in time for the World Cup. The 34-year-old thug, known as Gilly, headed a gang in Wolverhampton and said: "Fighting's what I live for. It's a way of life and I love it." He added: "I can't talk [to you] about my plans for the World Cup. If you put that in the paper then the police will be down here. That would mean £3,000 of my money down the drain." Shaw had been planning his trip to the finals in Japan and South Korea for months. Under new legislation aimed at stamping out football violence, police had the power to stop him and yobs like him from travelling abroad – but they had to catch them trying to leave the country. Arrogant Shaw couldn't resist bragging about how he enjoyed playing cat-and-mouse with the police and how he was determined to get to Japan. He said he had travelled to overseas internationals in the past, flying from Scottish airports or going by ferry to throw police off the scent. When asked by the *Mirror* about his criminal record for hooliganism, Shaw said: "I've been done for hooliganism more times than anyone else in Britain." He then demanded cash in return for his story – the *Mirror* refused to pay. Shaw boasted: "I've been a football hooligan for more than 20 years. Sometimes when we go away, we'll spend up to five months planning for it."

Just a few weeks later, former soccer hooligan Chris "Combat" Henderson was stopped trying to enter Japan to watch England v Argentina. He was held in Tokyo airport after flying from Bangkok and faced deportation to Thailand, where he ran a bar for Chelsea fans with Steve "The General" Hickmott, fellow ex-member of the Chelsea Headhunters. Also, Mark Morris, 40, of Manchester, Stephen Rimmer, 43, of Burnley and Eamonn Payne, 34, of Tipton, West Midlands, were arrested in Sapporo on suspicion of using forged US dollars.

In mid-June 2002, a postal worker sacked for football hooliganism was poised to receive a £125,000 pay-off. The decision marked a desperate attempt by Consignia (as the Post Office was known for a time) to draw a line under the case, which threatened to start a crippling strike. Mick Doherty and brother Tom were sacked for fighting at the 2000 UEFA Cup final between Arsenal and Turkey's Galatasaray. They won unfair dismissal cases. Tribunals ruled they should be reinstated but bosses refused and a two-year legal battle ensued. Postal workers in London threatened action and it was felt better to pay Mick Doherty off. Doherty said: "I can't say anything that will jeopardize ongoing negotiations."

In October 2002, Everton considered banning for life a football thug who had written a book about his exploits. Season-ticket holder Andy Nicholls had been arrested 19 times for soccer-related violence. In his book, he bragged that he is known to police across Europe but was only imprisoned once. He also detailed how he plotted with other Everton yobs to slash the face of Vinny Jones with a knife after a game at Goodison Park in 1994. Although the planned attack never took place, the allegations came amidst fears that the trouble that took place in Slovakia the previous weekend would mean that England would never be able to rid itself of hooligan followers. Club officials were unsurprisingly angry with Nicholls – who, as a category C hooligan, was among one of the worst offenders and had managed to dodge the checks and secure his season ticket. Merseyside police also launched an inquiry into his activities.

2003 – UEFA's Reputation in Tatters

UEFA's credibility was in tatters on 4th July 2003 after a laughable response to the disgraceful scenes that marred Turkey's Euro 2004 qualifier with Macedonia. European football's governing body was roundly criticized when it fined England a mere £68,000 for the pitch invasion and racism during the game against the Turks at Sunderland in April that year. UEFA had promised that it would come down hard on all hooliganism, in a determined attempt to rid the game of the problem. But faced with its first test since Macedonian players were struck by missiles after daring to score in Istanbul the month before, the guardians of the European game bottled it yet again.

Macedonia midfielder Sasko Lazarevski had his head cut open by a coin, while Turkish police had to raise their riot shields to protect visiting players as they took corners. Yet instead of ordering the Turks to play their next home match – England's vital Group 7 visit in October – behind closed doors, UEFA imposed a pathetic fine of just £22,000.

It was a decision that made a mockery of UEFA's claims to be leading the fight against hooliganism. While the FA was reluctant to become embroiled – aware any comment could inflame the tense relationship between English and Turkish fans – there was disappointment that UEFA had failed to take decisive action. The FA had already reduced its allocation of tickets for the match but there were genuine fears over the safety of Sven-Göran Eriksson's men in what was likely to be the most hostile and intimidating atmosphere any of them had encountered. While UEFA tried to justify their sentence, England fans' representatives pointed out how nonsensical it was. All commentators said that if England had to pay the price for its fans' behaviour, then surely other nations did too? UEFA had missed the chance to make a statement of intent. Any injury to England players would have to rest on their conscience.

2004 – Girl of 14 Imprisoned

On 2nd July 2004, a girl of 14 became Britain's first female soccer hooligan to be locked up. She was also the youngest to be convicted. Felicity Thorpe was sent to a detention centre for eight months for hurling up to 20 missiles at police in a riot after a Premiership game. Before being taken to the cells, she whispered with head bowed: "I'm sorry for what I've done." Pony-tailed Thorpe, who sat in court nervously nibbling her nails, was also banned from football grounds for six years. She admitted violent disorder. Her divorced mum, Annie, 50, said later: "My daughter is not a monster or a thug. It's true that she's becoming uncontrollable. But when she's not being naughty she's a real softie."

She admitted Thorpe was taken into care 15 months earlier because her behaviour "spiraled downwards". The teenage Portsmouth fan was captured on CCTV running amok after her team's home victory over Southampton in March 2004. At her side was a boy of 10 from her care home. The youngster – who could not be named for legal reasons – had already been handed a referral order for his part in the rioting, becoming Britain's youngest football hooligan. In three hours of violence, the two children were seen ducking under rope thugs tied across the road so they could not be charged by mounted police. They then pelted officers with stones. Thorpe, of Southsea, Hampshire, regularly vanished from view to rearm herself. When police called to interview her at her care home she was wearing the latest England shirt. Acting Detective Sergeant Gary Cable said: "It was surprising to see her caught up in the trouble. All the other offenders we saw were men. She didn't hurl just one missile. She was recorded as throwing between 15 and 20. That was a lot more than were thrown by men who have been jailed over this incident. She obviously had a clear disregard for the safety of police and public. But, when we questioned her, she admitted straightaway what she'd done."

After watching CCTV footage of the thuggery, magistrates' chairman, Paul Thompson, told Thorpe at Portsmouth court: "We're very concerned about you ... This offence is so serious only a custodial sentence is appropriate. You need to understand the community of which you are a part will not put up with this sort of behaviour." Only five out of more than 2,300 football banning orders involve women. The previous youngest offender was 16. Thorpe was held during Operation Market, which had been launched to net those involved in the violence. A 300-strong mob who tried to attack Southampton fans turned on police after being prevented from reaching its targets. In running battles, officers and their dogs and horses were injured, cars trashed and shops looted. At the time of the article about Thorpe, 47 hooligan supporters had been convicted.

2010 – MacIntyre "Bar Fight"

There were many more incidents of football hooliganism throughout the first decade of the 21st century.

In October 2010 undercover investigator, Donal MacIntyre was attacked after lunging at a man in a bar, a jury heard. James Wild, 47, claimed he was acting in self-defence. He was on trial for being part of a vengeance attack on MacIntyre, 44, and his wife Ameera. Wild's daughter, Caley Wild, 25, was also accused of assaulting the couple as payback for the reporter's 1999 documentary, which led to a six-year jail sentence for football hooligan Jason Marriner, from the Chelsea Headhunters gang. Wild, from Chertsey, Surrey, told Guildford Crown Court: "I acted 100% in self-defence. He lunged at me after he had been shouting 'come on then, come on'." Both MacIntyre and his wife were hurt in the alleged attack at a bar in Hampton Court, Surrey, in June 2010. Wild and his daughter both denied assault.

201... and Finally ... Football Hooligan Becomes a Woman

A self-confessed football hooligan underwent a sex change to become a woman. Twenty-four-stone Richard Allen, 36, lived for beating up rival fans at England, Spurs and Exeter City games – but changed his ways, and his body, and started living as Becci. Becci said: "If there was an Exeter City–Plymouth Argyle game we would just go down there and basically beat the crap out of whoever was supporting Argyle. To be honest, I only did a few games at City but I was a bigger England fan – beating up the Swedes was good fun." However, 6ft 2in Becci, showed violence the red card, lost seven stone in weight and became the woman she wanted to be. She still goes to darts and football, although she hadn't been to Exeter's ground for a while because of all the previous trouble she'd been in as a man. The Homebase worker said she knew from the age of eight she wanted to be a woman. Rather than explore her feminine side, she surrounded herself with tough friends and behaved as "manly" as possible to release her pent-up anger. It led to becoming a football hooligan.